Collins

GAA
Quiz Book

Dáire Brennan

Published by Collins
An imprint of
HarperCollins Publishers
Westerhill Road
Bishopbriggs
Glasgow G64 2QT
www.harpercollins.co.uk

First Edition 2014

10 9 8 7 6 5 4 3 2 1

ISBN 978-0-00-755009-8

Collins® is a registered trademark of
HarperCollins Publishers Limited

www.harpercollins.co.uk

Typeset by Davidson Publishing
Solutions, Glasgow

Printed in Great Britain by Clays Ltd,
St Ives plc

A catalogue record for this book is
available from the British Library.

If you would like to comment on any
aspect of this book, please contact us
at the above address or online.
E-mail: puzzles@harpercollins.co.uk

AUTHOR
Dáire Brennan

Forword

I wonder who played at midfield when ...?

Human beings by nature are inquisitive. The trait manifests itself in early childhood and often intensifies with the passing years. It was inevitable then that sources of information became a necessity and many of them have come in the hallowed form of a book. The latest comes from the wonderful world of Gaelic Games.

I'm sure many of you are aware of the fact that Gaelic Games and indeed Sports of all types with the exception of Archery were banned by Statute for an approximate five hundred years. That strange law held for England, Ireland, Scotland and Wales but like some other laws ways were found to engage in the 'evil' pastime of sport. The Statute was eventually repealed in the mid 1840s and ever since then organised sport has been on a steep upward curve. By degrees Unions, Associations, Leagues among other Titles emerged catering for competitions, contests and engagements for devotees of many sports.

Cumann Lúthchleas Gael or the Gaelic Athletic Association emerged in 1884; only six men, among them a Rugby International responded to Michael Cusack's open invitation to a meeting in Thurles for the purpose of setting up such an organization.
"Bíonn gach tosnú lag" – every beginning is weak but before long enthusiasm for the infant of Thurles 'spread like a prairie fire' described so aptly by Cusack.

Gaelic Sports by their very essence engender great passion and loyalty and that in turn provides debate, argument and sometimes unanswered questions. There are times when even the word of an accepted 'expert' would fail to solve a conundrum that might surface unexpectedly. That is where a book of a certain ilk comes to the rescue. If caught in that kind of a situation all you need do is state with authority that the answer can be found in *Collins Unofficial GAA Quiz Book*. It is a wonderful addition to the library of Gaelic Games.

Mícheál Ó Muircheartaigh

Introduction

The GAA has long been a secret organization that the Irish have kept to themselves. Foreign onlookers are fascinated by the ancient game of hurling and bemused by Gaelic Football. An afternoon watching these games will show you the levels of skill, bravery, and determination that the players possess, but that is only part of the great GAA story. The men who established the Association in Thurles in 1884 could never have dreamt of the impact that it has had on every aspect of Irish life over the past 130 years. Wars have been fought, governments have fallen, there have been economic booms and busts, Troubles and Emergencies, emigration and immigration, but the GAA has remained at the core of Irish life throughout it all.

One question that you will not find in this book is 'Why do thousands of volunteers around the world give up their time promoting the association?' Coaching children, organizing matches, running clubs for twenty years may all be worth it, just to see your club or county finally make the breakthrough. It's an indescribable sacrifice that our ancestors made before us and that will continue being made long after we are gone. The GAA is at the core of Irish life; the country would be unimaginable without it. There are few places on earth that any Irish person would want to be other than in a packed Clones, Thurles, or Croke Park for a championship battle in the middle of Summer, watching their county. Players such as Colm Cooper, Henry Shefflin, and Bernard Brogan are Irish heroes who are carrying on the legacy of Cú Chulainn, Na Fianna, and the thousands of other heroes who have played our games.

This book is for any GAA fan who fondly remembers great games, scores, and legends and who wants to test their knowledge.

Dáire Brennan

The quizzes

The book is divided into 100 different quizzes, split into three levels of difficulty. If you are a GAA diehard who never misses your county's games even in the depths of Winter, or if you a Summer follower who makes it only to the big games, there are quizzes that will suit you.

All aspects or football, hurling, ladies football, and camogie are covered right across the book, to ensure that you will find a quiz that will suit you.

Easy

The easy quizzes are like the pre-season competitions. Teams want to make a good start to the year. Games lack intensity, but you know that there will be trickier challenges right around the corner.

Medium

As the National Leagues start, managers want to fine-tune their teams and prepare for later on in the year. Games are getting harder and the standard is getting higher. You don't want to peak too soon, but you'll have to put in more of an effort.

Difficult

This is where you want to perform. All preparation has led to the Championship. This is where it counts and if you want to do well, you'll have to raise your game. There may be slip-ups and shocks along the way, but those who want to be crowned champions must do it at the top level.

The answers

The answers to each quiz are printed at the end of the following quiz. For example, the answers to Quiz 1-Pot Luck appear at the bottom of Quiz 2-Tour de France part 1. The exception to this rule is the last quiz in every level. The answers to these quizzes appear at the end of the very first quiz in the level.

Running a quiz

Every effort has been made to ensure that all the answers in the *Collins Unofficial GAA Quiz Book* are correct. Despite our best endeavours, mistakes may still appear. If you see an answer you are not sure is right, or if you think there is more than one possible answer, then check.

As any top player will tell you, every great performance requires preparation. The same goes for hosting a successful quiz. A little bit of effort beforehand will go a long way to making an event run smoothly. Plan your quiz, make sure that you have enough pens and paper, and be sure to ban smartphones.

Go n-éirí libh agus bain sult as an leabhar.

Contents

Easy Quizzes

Medium Quizzes

Difficult Quizzes

Easy Quizzes

Quiz 1: Pot Luck

1. Páirc Tailteann is the home ground of which county?

2. Which county has won the All-Ireland Football Championship the second most number of times?

3. Who managed Armagh to All-Ireland success in 2002?

4. Can you name the Donegal player who was awarded the All-Stars Player of the Year Award in 2012?

5. What colours are traditionally worn by Antrim?

6. Who won the 2014 All-Ireland Club Football Championship?

7. Who managed Clare to All-Ireland success in 2013?

8. In which year did Tyrone win the All-Ireland for the first time?

9. Which county won a three-in-a-row of All-Ireland Hurling titles during the 1970s?

10. Can you name the brothers who followed in their father's footsteps by winning an All-Ireland in 2011?

11. All-Ireland handball champion Robbie McCarthy is a native of which county?

12. Up to 2013, how many All-Stars has Colm Cooper won?

13. Apart from his native Clare, which other county has Davy Fitzgerald managed?

14. Which was the first county from north of the border to win the All-Ireland Senior Football Championship?

15. Name the Mayo native who managed Galway to two All-Ireland titles.

16. In which year did a Seamus Darby goal deny Kerry a five-in-a-row of All-Ireland Championships?

17. Which former Kilkenny hurler was known as 'The Dodger'?

18. Which county won the All-Ireland Minor Football Championship in 2001, 2004, 2008, and 2010?

19. Who captained Derry to All-Ireland success in 1993?
    a) Tony Scullion
    b) Henry Downey
    c) Joe Brolly

20. Which county has won the All-Ireland Camogie Championship the most times?
    a) Dublin
    b) Tipperary
    c) Cork

EASY

Answers to Quiz 33: Sponsors

1.	Antrim	11.	Meath
2.	Monaghan	12.	Kildare
3.	Cork	13.	Cork
4.	Kilkenny	14.	Tipperary
5.	Galway	15.	Dublin
6.	Sligo	16.	Offaly
7.	Westmeath	17.	Fermanagh
8.	Leitrim	18.	Waterford
9.	Meath	19.	Donegal
10.	Derry	20.	Laois

Quiz 2: Club Scene

In which county would you find the following clubs?

1. Pavee

2. Raparees

3. Kilmainhamwood

4. Crookedwood

5. Beragh Red Knights

6. Drung

7. Feale Rangers

8. Fighting Cocks

9. Magheracloone

10. Moy Davitts

11. Man-O-War

12. Burt

13. Modeligo

14. Hospital/Herbertstown

15. Liam Mellows

16. Aughawillian

17. Black and Whites

18. St. John Bosco

19. Courcey Rovers

20. Curry

Answers to Quiz 1: Pot Luck

1. Meath
2. Dublin
3. Joe Kernan
4. Michael Murphy
5. Saffron and white
6. St. Vincent's
7. Davy Fitzgerald
8. 2003
9. Cork
10. The Brogans
11. Westmeath
12. Eight
13. Waterford
14. Down
15. John O'Mahony
16. 1982
17. DJ Carey
18. Tyrone
19. b) Henry Downey
20. a) Dublin

Quiz 3: 1960s Football

1. Who was the Down captain who brought the Sam Maguire Cup across the border for the first time in 1960?

2. In which year did Offaly win its first ever Leinster Senior Championship?

3. Name the Down player who scored a goal directly from a line-ball in the 1960 All-Ireland Football Final.

4. A record attendance of 90,556 people was in Croke Park for the All-Ireland Final of which year?

5. Who scored a goal for Kerry after 34 seconds in the 1962 All-Ireland Final?

6. How many Ulster titles did Cavan win during the 1960s?

7. How many National League titles did Down win during the 1960s?

8. To whom did All-Ireland champions Dublin lose in the League Final of 1964?

9. Which number did Galway star Enda Colleran wear on his back during the All-Ireland Finals of 1963, 1964, 1965, and 1966?

10. Which All-Ireland-winning captain's father died during a final in the 1960s?

11. Who was the Kerry goalkeeper who made a number of important saves in the 1969 All-Ireland Final against Offaly?

12. In which year was the All-Ireland Final first broadcast live on television?

13. The 'Man in the Cap' famously coached Meath to All-Ireland success in 1967. What was his real name?

14. Name the St. Vincent's brothers who lined out for Dublin in the 1963 All-Ireland Final.

15. Who was the only player to be awarded the Texaco Footballer of the Year Award twice during the 1960s?

16. Which midlands county won its only National Football League title in 1966?

17. Meath defeated Cork on a scoreline of 1–9 to 0–9 in the 1967 All-Ireland Final. Who scored the important goal for the Royals?

18. Goalkeeper Willie Nolan captained Offaly in the All-Ireland Final of 1961, but later won a National League title in 1967 with which other team?

19. How many Munster Championships did Kerry win during the 1960s?
    a) 6
    b) 7
    c) 8

20. How many All-Ireland Senior Football titles did Dublin win during the 1960s?
    a) 1
    b) 2
    c) 3

Answers to Quiz 2: Club Scene

1. Dublin	11. Dublin
2. Wexford	12. Donegal
3. Meath	13. Waterford
4. Westmeath	14. Limerick
5. Tyrone	15. Galway
6. Cavan	16. Leitrim
7. Kerry	17. Kilkenny
8. Carlow	18. Down
9. Monaghan	19. Cork
10. Mayo	20. Sligo

Quiz 4: 1960s Hurling

1. Who was the Kilkenny man who captained Wexford to the All-Ireland title in 1960?

2. How many All-Irelands did Cork win during the 1960s?

3. Which Tipperary sharp-shooter scored a hat-trick in the 1964 All-Ireland Final?

4. Can you name the Wexford man who won an All-Ireland medal as a player in 1960, and later coached his county to All-Ireland success in 1968?

5. How many Munster Final appearances did Limerick make during the 1960s?

6. Which county lost an All-Ireland Final during the 1960s despite scoring six goals in the decider?

7. In which year during the 1960s did the All-Ireland champions fail to score a goal in the final?

8. Who lifted the Liam MacCarthy Cup twice as captain during the 1960s?

9. Who was the Kilkenny coach during the 1960s?

10. Can you name the Kilkenny player who captained his county to All-Ireland success in 1969?

11. In which year did Christy Ring play his last championship game for Cork?

12. Two players were sent off during the 1961 All-Ireland Final. Name them.

13. Against which county did Galway record its first victory in the Munster Championship in 1961?

14. In which year did Waterford win its first National Hurling League title?

15. How many Munster Championships did Tipperary win during the 1960s?

16. Name the Tipperary player, with eight All-Ireland medals, who retired after losing the 1967 All-Ireland Final.

17. Can you name the famous Thomastown native who played in goals for Kilkenny in five All-Ireland Finals during the 1960s?

18. Noel Drumgoole captained which county in an All-Ireland Final during the 1960s?

19. How many Munster titles did Waterford win during the 1960s?
    a) 1
    b) 2
    c) 3?

20. Wexford beat Tipperary in the 1968 Final by two points. By how many points were the Slaneysiders behind at half-time?
    a) 6
    b) 8
    c) 10

Answers to Quiz 3: 1960s Football

1. Kevin Mussen
2. 1960
3. Dan McCartan
4. 1961
5. Garry McMahon
6. Four
7. Three
8. New York City
9. 2
10. John Donnellan (in 1964)
11. Johnny Culloty
12. 1962
13. Peter McDermott
14. Lar and Des Foley
15. James McCartan (Down)
16. Longford
17. Terry Kearns
18. New York
19. c) 8
20. a) 1

Quiz 5: Football Managers

EASY

1. Who is the only Longford man to manage a county to All-Ireland success?

2. Name the former All-Star who managed St. Brigid's to All-Ireland Club Championship success in 2013.

3. Who managed Dublin to All-Ireland success in 2011?

4. Can you name the former All-Ireland winner who managed Derry to Ulster Championship success in 1998?

5. Name the intercounty manager who has managed Clare, Fermanagh, and Roscommon.

6. Who succeeded Jason Ryan as Wexford manager in 2012?

7. Which county did former Kildare player Glenn Ryan manage until 2013?

8. Who managed Mayo in the 2006 All-Ireland Football Final?

9. Current Kildare manager Jason Ryan played intercounty football with which county?

10. Who managed Offaly to Leinster success in 1997?

11. Former Down All-Ireland-winning manager Pete McGrath became manager of which county in 2013?

12. Can you name the only Derry man to manage a county to All-Ireland success?

13. Intercounty manager John Evans is a native of which county?

14. Who managed Tyrone directly before Mickey Harte took charge in 2002?

15. How many All-Ireland Championships did Billy Morgan win as Cork manager?

EASY

16. Name the Monaghan man who took charge of Meath during the 2010s.

17. In which year did Mick O'Dywer win his first All-Ireland as Kerry manager?

18. Name the man who was elected to the Dáil in 2011 while still an intercounty manager.

19. To how many All-Ireland Finals has Mickey Harte guided Tyrone?
    a) 2
    b) 3
    c) 4

20. Who managed Dublin to All-Ireland success in 1974?
    a) Tony Hanahoe
    b) Kevin Heffernan
    c) Des Foley

Answers to Quiz 4: 1960s Hurling

1. Nick O'Donnell
2. One
3. Donie Nealon
4. Padge Kehoe
5. None
6. Waterford
7. 1961 (Tipperary)
8. Jimmy Doyle
9. Fr. Tommy Maher
10. Eddie Keher
11. 1962
12. Lar Foley (Dublin) and Tom Ryan (Tipperary)
13. Clare
14. 1963
15. Seven
16. John Doyle
17. Ollie Walsh
18. Dublin
19. a) 1
20. b) 8

Quiz 6: Hurling Managers

1. Who was the Clare manager before Davy Fitzgerald took over in 2011?

2. How many All-Ireland titles did Fr. Tommy Maher win as Kilkenny coach?

3. Which county did former Offaly hurler Michael Duignan manage from 2001 to 2003?

4. Name the Kilkenny All-Ireland winner who became Dublin Under-21 manager in 2012.

5. In which year did Cyril Farrell become Galway senior hurling manager for the first time?

6. Who managed Kilkenny to All-Ireland successes in 1992 and 1993?

7. Name the Kilkenny man who managed a different county to All-Ireland success during the 1980s.

8. Before Michael Ryan in 2011, who was the last Waterford man to manage his native county?

9. Anthony Daly has managed a club to a county championship in which county?

10. Who managed Tipperary in the 2011 All-Ireland hurling final?

11. Who managed Cork to All-Ireland success in 1990?

12. Name the man who has managed the Kerry, Wexford, and Carlow senior hurling teams.

13. With which county did Anthony Cunningham begin his intercounty management career?

14. Who was the Cork manager during the first player's strike in 2002?

15. Who was the Kilkenny hurling manager before Brian Cody?

16. How many Munster titles did Ger Loughnane win as Clare hurling manager?

17. Former Waterford hurler Paul Flynn joined the management team of which county in 2013?

18. Name the Offaly man who managed Limerick during the 2000s.

19. Up to 2013, how many All-Ireland titles has Brian Cody won as Kilkenny manager?
    a) 8
    b) 9
    c) 10

20. Antrim manager Kevin Ryan is a native of which county?
    a) Wexford
    b) Carlow
    c) Waterford

Answers to Quiz 5: Football Managers

1. Eugene McGee
2. Kevin McStay
3. Pat Gilroy
4. Brian Mullins
5. John Maughan
6. Aidan O'Brien
7. Longford
8. Mickey Moran
9. Waterford
10. Tommy Lyons
11. Fermanagh
12. Éamonn Coleman
13. Kerry
14. Art McRory and Eugene McKenna
15. Two
16. Séamus McEnaney
17. 1975
18. Peter Fitzpatrick
19. b) 3
20. b) Kevin Heffernan

Quiz 7: 1970s Football

1. Who scored a hat-trick of goals for Kerry in the 1978 All-Ireland Final?

2. Which county won its provincial championship in 1975 for only the second time?

3. Can you name the Offaly player who scored his side's decisive goal in the 1971 All-Ireland Final?

4. In which year was the first 80-minute All-Ireland Final played?

5. How many Munster Championships did Cork win during the 1970s?

6. Can you name the Cork goalkeeper who lifted the Sam Maguire Cup as captain of his side in 1973?

7. Which Dublin forward won the coveted Texaco Footballer of the Year Award twice in the 1970s?

8. Name the Antrim player who selected as right corner-forward on the inaugural All-Star team in 1971.

9. Which Kerry player deputized for captain Mickey Ned O'Sullivan and lifted the Sam Maguire Cup after the 1975 All-Ireland Final?

10. Who managed Dublin to All-Ireland success in 1977?

11. How many All-Ireland medals did future soccer star Kevin Moran win during the 1970s?

12. In which year did Donegal win its first Ulster Championship?

13. Who captained Armagh in the 1977 All-Ireland Final?

14. Name the Kerry player who was sent off during the 1979 All-Ireland Final.

15. In which year during the 1970s was the All-Ireland Final settled after a replay?

16. Which county did Kerry defeat in the 1970 All-Ireland Final?

17. How many goals did Kerry score against Clare during their Munster Championship match in 1979?

18. Which Kerry great realeased a book in 1974 entitled *A Kerry Footballer*?

19. How many times did a team from Ulster play in an All-Ireland Final during the 1970s?
    a) 1
    b) 2
    c) 3

20. Which Galway player had his penalty saved by the Dublin goalkeeper in the 1974 All-Ireland Final?
    a) Liam Sammon
    b) Jimmy Duggan
    c) Colie McDonagh

Answers to Quiz 6: Hurling Managers

1. Ger O'Loughlin	11. Fr. Michael O'Brien
2. Seven	12. John Meyler
3. Meath	13. Roscommon
4. John Henderson	14. Bertie Óg Murphy
5. 1979	15. Kevin Fennelly
6. Ollie Walsh	16. Three
7. Diarmuid Healy	17. Down
8. Tony Mansfield	18. Pad Joe Whelahan
9. Kerry	19. b) 9
10. Declan Ryan	20. c) Waterford

Quiz 8: 1970s Hurling

1. Name the Limerick captain who lifted the Liam MacCarthy Cup after the 1973 All-Ireland Final.

2. In how many All-Ireland Finals did Wexford appear during the 1970s?

3. Who managed Cork to a 'three-in-a-row' of All-Ireland titles during the 1970s?

4. In which year did armed robbers steal £24,579 from the Semple Stadium gate receipts during the second half of a Munster Final?

5. How many goals did Limerick score in the 1973 Munster Hurling Final?

6. In which year was the All-Ireland Final broadcast in colour for the first time?

7. Can you name the Cork forward who scored his side's only goal during the 1978 All-Ireland Final?

8. In which year did Páirc Uí Chaoimh host the Munster Hurling Final for the first time?

9. Who was the Cork corner-forward who scored a hat-trick of goals during the 1970 All-Ireland Final?

10. Which future GAA official refereed the 1971 All-Ireland Final?

11. Name the Kilkenny forward who scored 2–11 in the 1971 All-Ireland Final.

12. Who captained Wexford in its All-Ireland defeats of 1976 and 1977?

13. Which county won its second and third National League titles in 1977 and 1978?

14. In which year did Brian Cody win his first All-Ireland medal as a player?

15. Who was the Tipperary player who played the final few minutes of the 1971 All-Ireland Final in his bare feet?

16. How many consecutive All-Star Awards did Kilkenny goalkeeper Noel Skehan win during the 1970s?

17. Can you name the Kilmacud Crokes hurler who won Dublin's first All-Star in 1971?

18. Who was the Limerick goalkeeper during the All-Ireland Finals of 1973 and 1974?

19. How many times did Kilkenny face Wexford in a Leinster Final during the 1970s?
    a) 8   b) 9   c) 10

20. How many times during the 1970s did a county score five goals in an All-Ireland Final and still end up losing the match?
    a) 3   b) 4   c) 5

EASY

Answers to Quiz 7: 1970s Football

1.	Eoin 'Bomber' Liston	11.	Two
2.	Sligo	12.	1972
3.	Murt Connor	13.	Jimmy Smyth
4.	1970	14.	Páidí Ó Sé
5.	Three	15.	1972
6.	Billy Morgan	16.	Meath
7.	Jimmy Keaveney	17.	Nine
8.	Andy McCallin	18.	Mick O'Connell
9.	Pat Spillane	19.	a) 1
10.	Tony Hanahoe	20.	a) Liam Sammon

Quiz 9: GAA Grounds

EASY

In which town would you find these GAA pitches?

1. Duggan Park

2. Celtic Park

3. Nowlan Park

4. Fraher Field

5. St. Brendan's Park

6. St. Tiernach's Park

7. St. Conleth's Park

8. Gaelic Park

9. O'Moore Park

10. MacHale Park

11. Páirc Esler

12. Brewster Park

13. McDonagh Park

14. Corrigan Park

15. Austin Stack Park

EASY

16. Dr. Cullen Park

17. St. Jarlath's Park

18. Pearse Park

19. MacCumhaill Park

20. Markievicz Park

Answers to Quiz 8: 1970s Hurling

1. Éamonn Grimes
2. Three
3. Fr. Bertie Troy
4. 1977
5. Six
6. 1971
7. Jimmy Barry-Murphy
8. 1976
9. Eddie O'Brien
10. Frank Murphy
11. Eddie Keher
12. Tony Doran
13. Clare
14. 1975
15. Michael 'Babs' Keating
16. Five
17. Mick Bermingham
18. Séamus Horgan
19. c) 10
20. a) 3

Quiz 10: Leinster Football Championship

1. Which is the only Leinster county never to have won the Leinster Football Championship?

2. Up to 2014, when is the last time that the Leinster Final went to a replay?

3. Which county did Laois defeat in the 2003 Leinster Football Final?

4. Where does Carlow play its home games in the Leinster Football Championship?

5. Before 2014, when did Dublin last play a Leinster Championship match outside of Croke Park?

6. After Dublin, which county has won the Leinster Championship on the most occasions?

7. True or false: 2004 was Westmeath's first appearance in a Leinster Final?

8. The Delaney Cup is named after brothers from which Leinster county?

9. Who managed Meath to Leinster success in 2010?

10. How many times did Dublin and Meath face each other in the Leinster Final during the 1990s?

11. Who captained Wexford in the 2011 Leinster Football Final?

12. Who is the last Dublin manager not to have won a Leinster Championship?

13. How many times did Mick O'Dwyer guide Kildare into a Leinster Final during his reign as manager?

14. Louth played three games in the Leinster Championship against which county in 2007?

15. The Leinster Final was has been played outside Croke Park once in the last hundred years. Where was the 1944 Leinster Final played?

16. In which year did Offaly beat neighbours Laois in the Leinster Final during the 1980s?

17. In which year did Longford last contest a Leinster Football Final?

18. How many counties has Luke Dempsey managed in the Leinster Football Championship?

19. Dublin beat which county by twenty-three points in the 2008 Leinster Football Final?
    a) Laois   b) Offaly   c) Wexford

20. How many Leinster titles did Seán Boylan win as Meath manager?
    a) 6   b) 8   c) 10

Answers to Quiz 9: GAA Grounds

1. Ballinasloe
2. Derry
3. Kilkenny
4. Dungarvan
5. Birr
6. Clones
7. Newbridge
8. New York
9. Portlaoise
10. Castlebar
11. Newry
12. Enniskillen
13. Nenagh
14. Belfast
15. Tralee
16. Carlow
17. Tuam
18. Longford
19. Ballybofey
20. Sligo

Quiz 11: Connacht Football Championship

EASY

1. Can you name the 1980s All-Ireland winner who won a Connacht Championship in 1985?

2. In what ground does New York play its home Connacht Championship matches?

3. Who was the first captain to be presented with the Nestor Cup during the 1950s?

4. Can you name the Leitrim player who was top scorer in the 2008 Connacht Football Championship?

5. Name the Roscommon player who scored the equalizing point from a long-range free in the 1991 Connacht Final.

6. With which other county did 1994 Leitrim captain Declan Darcy play?

7. How many counties has John O'Mahony managed to Connacht Championship success?

8. Who captained Sligo to Connacht Championship success in 2007?

9. Before 2010, when was the last time that a Connacht final did not feature either Galway or Mayo?

10. Can you name the Roscommon player who broke the crossbar during the 1992 Connacht Final?

11. In which decade did Roscommon last fail to win a Connacht Senior Football Championship?

12. Against which county did London record its first Connacht Championship victory in 1977?

13. How many Connacht counties has Derry native Mickey Moran managed?

14. In which year did Galway last complete a treble of Senior, Under-21, and Minor Connacht Championships?

15. Who scored three goals for Mayo in the 2013 Connacht Final?

16. Up to 2013, how many Connacht Championships has Sligo won?

17. In which year did New York bring Leitrim to extra time in their Connacht Championship meeting?

18. Up to 2013, who is the last Connacht player to win the All-Stars Footballer of the Year Award?

19. In which year was the Connacht Final last decided after a replay?
    a) 1989   b) 1995   c) 1998

20. How many Connacht Senior Championships did Mayo win during the 1980s?
    a) 3   b) 4   c) 5

Answers to Quiz 10: Leinster Football Championship

1.	Wicklow	11.	David Murphy
2.	2004	12.	Tommy Carr
3.	Kildare	13.	Five
4.	Dr. Cullen Park	14.	Wicklow
5.	2006	15.	Athy
6.	Meath	16.	1981
7.	False	17.	1968
8.	Laois	18.	Three
9.	Éamonn O'Brien	19.	c) Wexford
10.	Five	20.	b) 8

Quiz 12: 1980s Football

1. How many points did Tyrone full-forward Frank McGuigan score from play during the 1984 Ulster Final?

2. Who was the Offaly player who gave the long pass to Séamus Darby in the dying moments of the 1982 All-Ireland Final?

3. Name the Mayo player who scored his side's only goal during the 1989 All-Ireland Final.

4. In which year did Páidí Ó Sé captain the Kingdom to All-Ireland success?

5. Eugene McGee managed Offaly to All-Ireland success in 1982. What is Eugene's native county?

6. Who scored the important goal for Meath in the 1987 All-Ireland Final?

7. Which county won its first National League title in 1985?

8. Which county played in the All-Ireland Final for the first time in 1986?

9. Who was the Dublin captain who lifted the Sam Maguire Cup after the 1983 All-Ireland Final?

10. In which year did Seán Boylan become Meath manager?

11. Who succeeded Mick O'Dwyer as Kerry manager in 1989?

12. Between Nemo Rangers and St. Finbarr's, how many times did a Cork club win the All-Ireland Senior Club Championship during the 1980s?

13. Name the two Kildare-born players who won All-Ireland medals with Cork during the 1980s.

14. Which Cork player won his first Munster Championship in 1983 in his ninth attempt?

15. Who was the Antrim referee who sent off four players during the 1983 All-Ireland Final?

16. What colour jerseys did Kerry wear in the 1986 All-Ireland Semi-Final against Meath?

17. Which county won its first All-Ireland Under-21 Football Championship in 1982?

18. Who captained Roscommon in the 1980 All-Ireland Final?

19. Which county did Dublin beat in the 1985 Leinster Final?
a) Laois
b) Westmeath
c) Louth

20. How many All-Ireland titles did Kerry win during the 1980s?
a) 4
b) 5
c) 6

Answers to Quiz 11: Connacht Football Championship

1. Seán Lowry
2. Gaelic Park
3. Seán Purcell
4. Emlyn Mulligan
5. Derek Duggan
6. Dublin
7. Three
8. Noel McGuire
9. 1947
10. Enon Gavin
11. 1930s
12. Leitrim
13. Three
14. 2005
15. Cillian O'Connor
16. Three
17. 2012
18. Pádraic Joyce
19. c) 1998
20. b) 4

Quiz 13: 1980s Hurling

1. Who captained Kilkenny to All-Ireland success in 1982?

2. Can you name the Offaly player who won an All-Ireland hurling medal in 1981 before winning a football one the following year?

3. Which county did 1986 All-Star David Kilcoyne represent?

4. Who scored two goals for Cork in the 1986 All-Ireland Final against Galway?

5. Who was the Tipperary player who captained his side to Munster Senior Hurling Championship success 1987?

6. Galway bridged a gap of how many years by winning the All-Ireland in 1980?

7. Name the brothers from Borris-Ileigh who played in the 1989 All-Ireland Final.

8. Can you name the Kilkenny man who managed Offaly to All-Ireland success in 1981 and 1985?

9. Which county won its first All-Ireland Minor Championship in 1986?

10. Can you name the brothers who were selected to the GAA Team of the Century in 1984?

11. Where was the 1984 All-Ireland Hurling Final played?

12. Whichh county did Antrim defeat in the All-Ireland Semi-Final of 1989?

13. Can you name the Limerick full-forward who won his sixth consecutive All-Star award in 1981?

14. Who managed Galway to its three All-Ireland titles in the 1980s?

EASY

15. Which county did Galway defeat in the 1980 All-Ireland Final?

16. Which county did Offaly defeat in the 1985 Leinster Final?

17. Can you name the Clare goalkeeper who won an All-Star award in 1981?

18. 1982 All-Star Jim Greene played for which county?

19. How many All-Ireland titles did Kilkenny win during the 1980s?
    a) 2
    b) 3
    c) 4

20. Which song did Joe McDonagh sing from the Hogan Stand after Galway won the 1980 All-Ireland Final?
    a) 'Galway Bay'
    b) 'Fields of Athenry'
    c) 'The West's Awake'

Answers to Quiz 12: 1980s Football

1. Eleven
2. Liam Connor
3. Anthony Finnerty
4. 1985
5. Longford
6. Colm O'Rourke
7. Monaghan
8. Tyrone
9. Tommy Drumm
10. 1982
11. Mickey 'Ned' O'Sullivan

12. Eight
13. Shea Fahy and Larry Tompkins
14. Dinny Allen
15. John Gough
16. Blue
17. Donegal
18. Danny Murray
19. a) Laois
20. b) 5

Quiz 14: Sponsors

Which county has each of these companies sponsored?

1. Tommy Varden

2. Brady Ham

3. Lawlor's Hotel

4. Sports Savers

5. Eircell

6. Glennon Brothers

7. Genfitt

8. Investec

9. Kingspan

10. Boylesports

11. Skoda

12. Masonite

13. WJ Dolan

14. MW Hire

15. Brennanhotels.com

EASY

16. Bewley's Hotel

17. Specialist Joinery

18. 747 Travel

19. Shaw's

20. Canal Court Hotel

Answers to Quiz 13: 1980s Hurling

1. Brian Cody
2. Liam Currams
3. Westmeath
4. Kevin Hennessy
5. Richie Stakelum
6. 57
7. Bobby and Aidan Ryan
8. Dermot Healy
9. Offaly
10. Nicky and Bobby Rackard
11. Semple Stadium
12. Offaly
13. Joe McKenna
14. Cyril Farrell
15. Limerick
16. Laois
17. Séamus Durack
18. Waterford
19. a) 2
20. c) 'The West's Awake'

Quiz 15: Munster Hurling

1. Kerry has won one game in the Munster Senior Championship since 1926. Which county did it beat?

2. Which county won a Munster Final during the 1960s by only scoring 11 points?

3. Can you name the Cork player who has won ten Munster Senior Hurling Championships?

4. Where did the 1987 Munster Final replay between Cork and Tipperary take place?

5. Who managed Clare in the 1993 and 1994 Munster Finals?

6. In which year did John Fenton score a goal from forty-five yards out in the Munster Championship?

7. Which Cork player was sent off in the 2013 Munster Senior Final?

8. Who knocked subsequent All-Ireland Champions Clare out of the 2013 Munster Championship?

9. Can you name the Limerick player who scored two goals in the 1996 Munster Final replay?

10. Which was the first county to win the All-Ireland after losing the Munster Final?

11. Who captained his county to three Munster Championships during the 1990s?

12. By what name was Semple Stadium known before 1971?

13. How many Munster champions have gone on to win the All-Ireland since 2000?

14. In which year did Brendan Cummins make his Munster Championship debut for Tipperary?

15. Can you name the former All-Ireland winner who has managed four counties in the Munster Championship?

16. Who scored three goals in a Munster Final but still lost during the 2000s?

17. Who managed Waterford to Munster Championship success in 2010?

18. How many Munster Finals did Ger Loughnane lose as a player for Clare?

19. Which one of these Munster greats has won the most Munster Championship medals?
    a) John Doyle
    b) Mick Mackey
    c) Christy Ring

20. How many goals did Tipperary score in the 2011 Munster Final against Waterford?
    a) 6
    b) 7
    c) 8

Answers to Quiz 14: Sponsors

1. Galway	11. Tipperary
2. Kildare	12. Leitrim
3. Waterford	13. Tyrone
4. Wexford	14. Laois
5. Clare	15. Wicklow
6. Longford	16. London
7. Mayo	17. Derry
8. Monaghan	18. Roscommon
9. Cavan	19. Limerick
10. Louth	20. Down

Quiz 16: 1990s Football

EASY

1. Can you name the Tyrone player who scored 11 of his side's 12 points in the 1995 All-Ireland Final?

2. Which county won the Munster Championship for only the second time in its history in 1992?

3. In which year during the 1990s did Armagh win its first Ulster title since 1982?

4. Which club in 1990 became the first Wicklow club to win the All-Ireland Club Championship?

5. Can you name the Royal county ace who scored the winning point against Dublin in his fourth game in the 1991 Leinster Championship?

6. Which county did Kildare defeat in the 1998 Leinster Final?

7. Who in 1998 became Tipperary's first football All-Star?

8. Can you name the Down footballer who followed in his father's footsteps by winning the All-Ireland during the 1990s?

9. Who was the only Leitrim player to be awarded with an All-Star following the county's Connacht Championship victory in 1994?

10. Who managed Dublin in the 1992 All-Ireland Football Final?

11. Who was full-back on the Derry All-Ireland-winning team of 1993?

12. Can you name the referee who sent off Liam McHale and Colm Coyle in the 1996 All-Ireland Final?

13. Can you name the Mayo player who scored a penalty in the 1997 All-Ireland Final?

14. How many Ulster titles did Down win during the 1990s?

15. The documentary *A Year Til Sunday* followed which All-Ireland-winning county during the 1990s?

16. In which year was Tony Davis sent off during the All-Ireland Final?

17. Who was the Dublin All-Ireland-winning manager in 1995?

18. Which county won the National Football League on three occasions during the 1990s?

19. Which one of these 1990s All-Ireland-winning captains has never run for election to Dáil Éireann?
    a) John O'Leary
    b) Graham Geraghty
    c) Anthony Molloy

20. How many Ulster titles did Donegal win during the 1990s?
    a) 1
    b) 2
    c) 3

Answers to Quiz 15: Munster Hurling

1. Waterford
2. Waterford (1963)
3. Jimmy Barry-Murphy
4. Fitzgerald Stadium
5. Len Gaynor
6. 1987
7. Pat Horgan
8. Cork
9. Owen O'Neill
10. Cork (2004)
11. Anthony Daly
12. Thurles Sportsfield
13. Two
14. 1995
15. Justin McCarthy
16. John Mullane
17. Davy Fitzgerald
18. Five
19. a) John Doyle
20. b) 7

Quiz 17: 1990s Hurling

EASY

1. How many counties won the All-Ireland Senior Hurling Championship during the 1990s?

2. How many All-Ireland Finals did Limerick lose in the 1990s?

3. Which 1996 hurling song knocked the Spice Girls off the top of the charts?

4. Who scored Wexford's only goal in the 1996 All-Ireland Hurling Final?

5. How many All-Ireland Senior Hurling Championship Finals did DJ Carey play in during the 1990s?

6. Who was the Wexford goalkeeper in the 1996 All-Ireland Hurling Final?

7. Who was the inaugural All-Star Hurler of the Year in 1995?

8. Who managed Dublin in the Leinster Finals of 1990 and 1991?

9. Who were the three brothers who won an All-Ireland with Tipperary in 1991?

10. How many Munster Senior Hurling Championship Finals did Waterford play in during the 1990s?

11. Who became the first Down hurler to win an All-Star in 1992?

12. How many Leinster Senior Hurling Championships did Wexford win during the 1990s?

13. Who was the only man to lift the Liam MacCarthy cup on two occasions as All-Ireland-winning captain during the 1990s?

14. Can you name the Kilkenny club that won the All-Ireland Club Hurling Championship in 1991?

15. Which author wrote the book *Hurling, The Revolutionary Years* in 2005?

16. By how many points were Clare leading when their All-Ireland Semi-Final replay against Offaly in 1998 was prematurely ended?

17. Which 1990s All-Ireland Hurling Final failed to produce a goal?

18. Who captained Offaly to All-Ireland success in 1994?

19. How many senior hurling managers did Offaly have during the 1990s?
    a) 5
    b) 6
    c) 7

20. In which year was the 'back door' for beaten provincial finalists introduced in hurling?
    a) 1996
    b) 1997
    c) 1998

Answers to Quiz 16: 1990s Football

1. Peter Canavan
2. Clare
3. 1999
4. Baltinglass
5. David Beggy
6. Meath
7. Declan Browne
8. James McCartan
9. Séamus Quinn
10. Paddy Cullen
11. Tony Scullion
12. Pat McEnaney
13. Ciarán McDonald
14. Two
15. Galway
16. 1993
17. Pat O'Neill
18. Derry
19. c) Anthony Molloy
20. b) 2

Quiz 18: Club Scene

With which club do or did these hurlers play?

1. Tony Kelly

2. Willie O'Connor

3. Martin Hanamy

4. Tom Dempsey

5. Liam Watson

6. Conal Keaney

7. Tommy Dunne

8. Joe Connolly

9. Dan Shanahan

10. Joe Deane

11. Mick Mackey

12. Brian Lohan

13. Fergal Moore

14. JJ Delaney

15. Lar Corbett

EASY

16. Jack Guiney

17. Gary Kirby

18. Lar Foley

19. Shane Brick

20. Lorcán McLoughlin

Answers to Quiz 17: 1990s Hurling

1. Six
2. Two
3. Dancing at the Crossroads
4. Tom Dempsey
5. Five
6. Damien Fitzhenry
7. Brian Lohan
8. Lar Foley
9. Colm, Conal, and Cormac Bonnar
10. One (1998)

11. Gerard McGrattan
12. Two
13. Anthony Daly
14. Glenmore
15. Denis Walsh
16. Three
17. 1999
18. Martin Hanamy
19. c) Seven
20. b) 1997

Quiz 19: Who Said That?

Identify the person responsible for each of these quotations:

1. 'Keep your eye on the ball, even when it's in the referee's pocket.'

2. 'It's definitely probably one of the greatest days in Aherlow in GAA circumstances.'

3. 'There won't be a cow milked in Finglas tonight.'

4. 'I never retired. They just stopped picking me.'

5. 'If two poor teams are on a pitch and one is much fitter, that team will win.'

6. 'The only time in my playing days I heard anybody talking about hamstrings was when they were hanging outside a butcher's shop.'

7. 'Mickey Joe made his championship debut in such a way that he will never be asked to make it again.'

8. 'They were saying nice things to me – I preferred it when they hated me.'

9. 'If you are member of a certain political party and of the GAA, then you're shagged altogether.'

10. 'How can you talk logic and analyse a game when you're talking about Kildare?'

11. 'The more you get used to playing in Croke Park, the worse it gets.'

12. 'Games grow out of the soil, just as plants do. Hurling grew out of the soil of Ireland.'

13. 'And Tom Cheasty breaks through with Kilkenny defenders falling around him like dying wasps.'

14. 'I warned the boys they couldn't go through the league unbeaten and, unfortunately, they appear to have listened to me.'

15. 'They've lost nothing today – except pride and, of course, the Connacht title.'

16. 'The worst thing about the game was there wasn't even a chance of a row.'

17. 'You might be better off watching *Buffy the Vampire Slayer* on the other channel.'

18. 'Davey Forde wouldn't be a free-taker if you boiled him in a pot.'

19. 'What have Sinn Féin and Tyrone got in common? Sinn Féin have a better chance of seeing an All-Ireland.'

20. 'There is a level of politics in hurling. I don't think Henry Kissinger would have lasted a week in the Munster Council.'

Answers to Quiz 18: Club Scene

1. Ballyea
2. Glenmore
3. St. Rynagh's
4. Buffer's Alley
5. Loughiel Shamrocks
6. Ballyboden St. Enda's
7. Toomevara
8. Castlegar
9. Lismore
10. Killeagh
11. Ahane
12. Wolfe Tones na Sionna
13. Turloughmore
14. Fenians
15. Thurles Sarsfields
16. Rathnure
17. Patrickswell
18. St. Vincent's
19. Kilmoyley
20. Kanturk

Quiz 20: Nicknames

Identify the following GAA personalities by their nicknames:

1. Sparrow

2. Brick

3. Hopper

4. Chunky

5. Fat Larry

6. Ricey

7. The Gunner

8. Mugsy

9. Pillar

10. Star

11. Jigger

12. Beano

13. Geezer

14. Rasher

15. Smiley

16. Cake

17. Nuxer

18. Gizzy

19. Nudie

20. Wooly

Answers to Quiz 19: Who Said That?

1. Christy Ring
2. Eddie Moroney
3. Keith Barr
4. Tony Scullion
5. Kevin Heffernan
6. Mick 'Rattler' Byrne
7. John B Keane
8. Joe Brolly
9. Charlie McCreevy
10. Tony Davis
11. Páidí Ó Sé
12. Michael Cusack
13. Micheál O'Hehir
14. Art McRory
15. Marty Morrissey
16. Colm O'Rourke
17. Pat Spillane
18. Tom Ryan
19. Colm O'Rourke
20. Ger Loughnane

Quiz 21: 2000s Football

EASY

1. Can you name the Armagh player who was sent off in the 2003 All-Ireland Football Final?

2. In which year was the qualifier system brought into the All-Ireland Championship?

3. How many times did Tyrone beat Kerry in the Championship during the 2000s?

4. Name the Kerry footballer who scored five points in the 2002 All-Ireland Football Final.

5. In which round did Dublin play Kerry twice in Thurles during the 2001 All-Ireland Championship?

6. Who scored the winning point for Fermanagh against Armagh in the 2004 All-Ireland Quarter-Final?

7. In which year did Owen Mulligan score a famous goal against Dublin in an All-Ireland Quarter-Final?

8. Can you name the Laois captain who, in 2003, became the first man from the O'Moore County to lift the Leinster Championship trophy since 1946?

9. Can you name the brothers who both won the All-Stars Footballer of the Year Award during the 2000s?

10. Which county did Westmeath defeat after a replay in the 2004 Leinster Final?

11. Who were the inaugural winners of the Tommy Murphy Cup in 2004?

12. Which Ulster county won six Senior Ulster Football Championships during the 2000s?

13. Can you name the Dublin forward who hit the post with a last minute free against Armagh in the 2002 All-Ireland Semi-Final?

EASY

14. Who succeeded Páidí Ó Sé as Kerry football manager in 2003?

15. Which county won its first National Football League in 2007?

16. How many All-Ireland medals did Colm Cooper win during the 2000s?

17. Can you name the Mayo footballer who scored one goal in the 2006 All-Ireland Football Final?

18. Which county did Armagh defeat in the 2008 Ulster Final?

19. Can you name the Tyrone defender who made the famous block on Steven McDonnell in the 68th minute of the 2003 Final?
    a) Ciarán Gourley   b) Gavin Devlin   c) Conor Gormley

20. How many Leinster Championships did Dublin win during the 2000s?
    a) 6   b) 7   c) 8

Answers to Quiz 20: Nicknames

1. Ger O'Loughlin
2. Michael Walsh
3. Oliver McGrath
4. Liam O'Brien or Damian Hayes
5. Anthony Finnerty
6. Ryan McMenamin
7. Paul Brady
8. Owen Mulligan
9. Paul Caffrey
10. Kieran Donaghy
11. John O'Connor
12. Brian McDonald
13. Kieran McGeeney
14. Michael O'Brien
15. Derek O'Reilly
16. Shane Curran
17. Niall Buckley
18. Diarmuid Lyng
19. Eugene Hughes
20. Colm Parkinson

Quiz 22: 2000s Hurling

EASY

1. How many All-Ireland Finals did not feature Kilkenny during the 2000s?

2. Who managed Tipperary to All-Ireland success in 2001?

3. Which county won the National Hurling League in 2007, for the first time since 1963?

4. Which company sponsored the All-Ireland Championship from 1995 until 2008?

5. Name the Kilkenny player who scored 1–3 in the 2006 All-Ireland Hurling Final?

6. How many Leinster Senior Championships did Wexford win during the 2000s?

7. Can you name the Waterford player who scored a hat-trick against Cork in the 2003 Munster Final?

8. Which county won its first Under-21 All-Ireland title in 2009?

9. Who captained Cork to All-Ireland success in 2004?

10. Which county did Waterford beat in the 2008 All-Ireland Semi-Final?

11. In which year did DJ Carey win his last All-Ireland?

12. Who was the Laois player who scored 8–187 in Championship hurling during the 2000s?

13. How many All-Ireland Club Championships did Portumna win during the 2000s?

14. Who scored Offaly's only goal in the 2000 All-Ireland Final?

15. Can you name the Kilkenny player who won the All-Star Hurler of the Year Award in 2009?

16. Which county appeared in its first ever Leinster Minor Final in 2006?

17. Can you name the former Clare player who took charge of the Waterford hurling team midway through the 2008 Championship?

18. Who were the first winners of the Christy Ring Cup in 2005?

19. Can you name the Galway player who scored 2–9 in the 2005 All-Ireland Semi-Final against Kilkenny?
    a) Niall Healy
    b) Ger Farragher
    c) David Forde

20. In which year did Kilkenny defeat Limerick in the All-Ireland Final?
    a) 2007
    b) 2008
    c) 2009

Answers to Quiz 21: 2000s Football

1.	Diarmuid Marsden	11.	Clare
2.	2001	12.	Armagh
3.	Three	13.	Ray Cosgrove
4.	Dara Ó Cinnéide	14.	Jack O'Connor
5.	Quarter-Final	15.	Donegal
6.	Tom Brewster	16.	Four
7.	2005	17.	Pat Harte
8.	Ian Fitzgerald	18.	Fermanagh
9.	Tomás and Marc Ó Sé	19.	c) Conor Gormley
10.	Laois	20.	a) 6

Quiz 23: Munster Football Championship

1. Waterford won its first Munster Championship match in nineteen years in 2007 by beating which county?

2. Who captained Cork to Munster Championship success in 1993?

3. How many Munster Championships did Kerry win during the 1990s?

4. In which year did Pat Spillane win his final Munster Championship medal?

5. Who scored Kerry's only goal in the 2013 Munster Football Final?

6. Who scored Clare's winning goal against Cork in the 1997 Munster Championship?

7. Which Kerry player scored 2–4, the same amount as Cork, in the 1979 Munster Final?

8. Who managed Cork to Munster Championship success in 1983?

9. In which year did Tipperary last win the Munster Senior Football Championship?

10. Starting in 1958, how many consecutive Munster Championships did Kerry win?

11. Can you name the two midfielders who won a Club All-Ireland together as a pairing during the 1970s, and played against each other in a Munster Final?

12. Hennessy Memorial Park has hosted many Munster Championship games. Where is it located?

13. In which year did Séamus Moynihan make his Munster Championship debut?

14. Can you name the Kerry man who managed Limerick in the 2003 and 2004 Munster Finals?

EASY

15. The Munster Championship winning captains from 1960 to 1964 all came from which club?

16. True or false: the Munster Senior Championship Cup has no name?

17. Which county did Clare beat in the 2012 Munster Championship Semi-Final?

18. Can you name the former Cork All-Ireland winner who managed Waterford in the Munster Championship during the 2000s?

19. In which year did Darragh, Tomás, and Marc Ó Sé first win a Munster Championship together?
    a) 2000   b) 2002   c) 2004

20. How many Munster Championship medals did Billy Morgan win as a player?
    a) 5   b) 6   c) 7

Answers to Quiz 22: 2000s Hurling

1. Two
2. Nicky English
3. Waterford
4. Guinness
5. Aidan Fogarty
6. One
7. John Mullane
8. Clare
9. Ben O'Connor
10. Tipperary
11. 2003
12. James Young
13. Three
14. Johnny Pilkington
15. Tommy Walsh
16. Carlow
17. Davy Fitzgerald
18. Westmeath
19. b) Ger Farragher
20. a) 2007

Quiz 24: GAA Biographies

Identify the player who is the subject of these biographies:

1. *Hungry Hill*

2. *Back to the Hill*

3. *Triumph and Troubles*

4. *Lá an Phaoraigh*

5. *Tangled up in Blue*

6. *If you don't know me, don't judge me*

7. *Blessed and Obsessed*

8. *Keys to the Kingdom*

9. *All or Nothing*

10. *Come What May*

11. *Life, Death and Hurling*

12. *Without a Shadow of a Doubt*

13. *Every Single Ball*

14. *I Crossed the Line*

15. *Passion and Pride*

EASY

16. *Every Step We Took*

17. *The Gambler*

18. *The Right to Win*

19. *Out of our Skins*

20. *Unfinished Business*

Answers to Quiz 23: Munster Football Championship

1. Clare
2. Mick McCarthy
3. Four
4. 1991
5. Colm Cooper
6. Martin Daly
7. Ger Power
8. Éamonn Ryan
9. 1935
10. Eight
11. John O'Keeffe and Dinny Long
12. Milltown Malbay
13. 1992
14. Liam Kearns
15. John Mitchels
16. True
17. Limerick
18. Denis Walsh
19. c) 2004
20. a) 5

Quiz 25: Leinster Hurling

1. How many Leinster Senior Championship medals did Kilkenny player Michael Kavanagh win during his career?

2. Who scored Dublin's only goal in its 2013 defeat of Kilkenny in the Leinster Championship Semi-Final Replay?

3. Craig Doyle scored three goals in a Leinster Championship match in 2011 for which county?

4. How many Leinster Hurling Championships did Kilkenny win during the 2000s?

5. In which year did Offaly win the Leinster Championship for the first time?

6. Who captained Wexford to Leinster success in 1997?

7. Who knocked Dublin out of the 2006 Leinster Championship?

8. Can you name the hurler who scored a goal against his native county in the 1997 Leinster Championship?

9. Which county has won the Leinster Championship for the second-most number of times?

10. In which year during the 1990s did 55,492 people attend the Leinster Hurling Final?

11. Can you name the player who won twelve Leinster Championships for two different counties during his career?

12. Where were the 2002 Leinster Hurling Championship Semi-Finals played?

13. Can you name the father-son combination who managed and captained a team in the Leinster Championship during the 1990s?

14. How many Leinster Championships did Offaly win during the 1980s?

15. Can you name the brothers who both captained Kilkenny to Leinster Championship success during the 1970s?

16. Can you name the Offaly player who scored a hat-trick of goals against Kilkenny in the 1989 Leinster Championship?

17. Who was the last captain to lift the old Bob O'Keeffe Cup during the 2000s?

18. In which year were there twelve goals in the Leinster Final?

19. In 2012, a Leinster Senior Hurling Championship medal was sold on eBay for how much?
    a) €570
    b) €670
    c) €770

20. By how many points was Galway leading Kilkenny at half time in the 2012 Leinster Final?
    a) 10
    b) 12
    c) 14

Answers to Quiz 24: GAA Biographies

1. Pat Critchley
2. John O'Leary
3. Charlie Carter
4. Seán Óg de Paor
5. Dessie Farrell
6. Dan Shanahan
7. Mick O'Dwyer
8. Jack O'Connor
9. Terence 'Sambo' McNaughton
10. Dónal Óg Cusack
11. Michael Duignan
12. Joe Kernan
13. Brian Corcoran
14. Liam Dunne
15. Davy Fitzgerald
16. Peter Canavan
17. Oisín McConville
18. Cyril Farrell
19. Liam Hayes
20. Tadhg Kennelly

Quiz 26: Pot Luck

1. Who captained Wexford to All-Ireland success in 1996?

2. In which county would you find the club Ramor United?

3. In which year did Cork complete a double of football and hurling All-Ireland titles?

4. Who scored 2–3 in the 2013 All-Ireland Football Final?

5. Which Ulster county plays in green and white?

6. In which year did Brian Cody win his first All-Ireland as Kilkenny manager?

7. The Curse of Biddy Early was associated with which county?

8. Healy Park is the home ground of which county?

9. For which two counties did Declan Darcy play?

10. The Anglo-Celt Cup is presented to the winners of which provincial championship?

11. How many All-Ireland Hurling Championships did Galway win during the 1980s?

12. Tadhg O'Connor, Mick Murphy, and Matt Hassett all captained which county to All-Ireland success?

13. Mick Lawlor, Noel Garvan, and Aidan Fennelly won a provincial title with which county during the 2000s?

14. 'The Rose of Mooncoin' is the traditional song associated with which county?

15. Comedian Patrick Kielty played minor football for which county?

16. Who managed Kildare to the 1998 All-Ireland Football Final?

17. In which county does the All-Ireland Poc Fada Championship annually take place?

18. How many All-Ireland titles did Páidí Ó Sé win as a player?

19. In which year did Offaly win its first All-Ireland Hurling Championship?
    a) 1941
    b) 1961
    c) 1981

20. The Sheepstealers' is the nickname of which county?
    a) Longford
    b) Roscommon
    c) Leitrim

Answers to Quiz 25: Leinster Hurling

1. Thirteen
2. Danny Sutcliffe
3. Carlow
4. Nine
5. 1980
6. Rod Guiney
7. Westmeath
8. James 'Shiner' Brennan
9. Dublin
10. 1997
11. Matty Power
12. Semple Stadium
13. Ollie and Michael Walsh
14. Six
15. Pat and Ger Henderson
16. Mark Corrigan
17. John O'Connor
18. 1972
19. a) €570
20. c) 14

Quiz 27: Ulster Football Championship

1. Who is the all-time leading scorer in the Ulster Senior Football Championship?

2. How many Ulster Championships did Down win during the 1960s?

3. Can you name the two Tyrone players who were sent off in the 2005 Ulster Final Replay?

4. In which year did Donegal win the Ulster Championship for the first time?

5. Can you name the former All-Ireland-winning captain who managed two Ulster counties during the 2000s?

6. Can you name the county who had a point cancelled because the band was still on the pitch in an Ulster Final during the 1970s?

7. Which former All-Ireland winner managed Cavan to Ulster success in 1997?

8. How many Ulster Championships did Brian McEniff win as a player?

9. Which was the only Ulster county not to contest an Ulster Final during the 1980s?

10. Who was top scorer in the Ulster Championship in 2000, 2001, and 2002?

11. In which year did Fermanagh last appear in an Ulster Final?

12. Which county has won the Ulster Championship the second-most number of times?

13. Which county and in which year did the Ulster champions play in the preliminary round, for the first time since Cavan in 1945?

14. Pearse McKenna was sent off in the first minute of a 2004 Ulster Championship match while playing for which county?

15. Where does Down play its home games in the Ulster Championship?

16. How many Ulster Championships did Pete McGrath win as Down manager?

17. In which year did Antrim last win the Ulster Championship?

18. Can you name the player who played in the Ulster Minor Championship and Senior Championship on the same day in 2011?

19. How many Ulster Championships did Paul McGrane win during his Armagh career?
    a) 6   b) 7   c) 8

20. Which county did Antrim beat in the 2009 Ulster Championship Semi-Final?
    a) Down   b) Derry   c) Cavan

Answers to Quiz 26: Pot Luck

1. Martin Storey
2. Cavan
3. 1990
4. Bernard Brogan
5. Fermanagh
6. 2000
7. Clare
8. Tyrone
9. Leitrim and Dublin
10. Ulster
11. Three
12. Tipperary
13. Laois
14. Kilkenny
15. Down
16. Mick O'Dwyer
17. Louth
18. Eight
19. c) 1981
20. b) Roscommon

Quiz 28: Club Scene

With which club do or did these footballers play?

1. Leighton Glynn

2. Mike Frank Russell

3. Declan Browne

4. Dermot McCabe

5. Alan Brogan

6. Trevor Giles

7. Matt Connor

8. Glen Ryan

9. Billy Morgan

10. Anthony Tohill

11. Liam McHale

12. Declan Bonner

13. Eugene Hughes

14. Steven McDonnell

15. Dessie Dolan

16. Dan Gordon

17. Mattie Forde

18. Seán Óg De Paor

19. Peter Canavan

20. Dermot Earley Snr.

Answers to Quiz 27: Ulster Football Championship

1. Oisín McConville
2. Six
3. Stephen O'Neill and Peter Canavan
4. 1972
5. Paddy O'Rourke
6. Donegal
7. Martin McHugh
8. Two
9. Antrim
10. Rory Gallagher
11. 2008
12. Monaghan
13. Armagh in 2005
14. Cavan
15. Páirc Esler
16. Two
17. 1951
18. Paddy McBrearty
19. b) 7
20. c) Cavan

Quiz 29: GAA Books

EASY

1. Enda McEvoy's book *The Godfather of Modern Hurling* chronicles the career of which All-Ireland-winning coach?

2. *My Journey* recalls the life and career of which former dual-code athlete?

3. Can you name the GAA historian who wrote the books *Lest we Forget*, *The Throw-In*, and *Legends of the Ash*?

4. *Rebel Rebel* tells the story of which former Cork player?

5. Can you name the photography agency which annually releases a pictorial book of the GAA year called *A Season of Sundays*?

6. Which club does Christy O'Connor focus on in his book *The Club*?

7. Who wrote the book *How the GAA Survived the Troubles*?

8. Which period does Denis Walsh's *Hurling, The Revolutionary Years* chronicle?

9. The book *Rucks, Mauls and Gaelic Football* is about which former footballer and rugby player?

10. The book *Working on a Dream* followed which intercounty football team for a year?

11. *A Parish far from Home* tells the story of the GAA club in which European capital city?

12. Which was the first GAA-related book to win the William Hill Irish Sports Book of the Year Award?

13. Which GAA personality wrote the book *From Borroloola to Mangerton Mountain*?

14. The book *House of Pain* tells the story of which county?

15. Which former All-Ireland winner wrote a biography of Kevin Heffernan entitled *Heffo, A Brilliant Mind*?

16. *Kings of September* is an account of the build-up and the All-Ireland Final of which year?

17. Which former Kerry great wrote a book entitled *How to play Gaelic Football*?

18. Can you name the All-Ireland winner who was awarded a PhD following research that included a thesis entitled *Towards a Philosophy for Legislation in Gaelic Games*?

19. Can you name the RTÉ broadcaster who annually releases a book with statistics on that year's championship?
    a) Des Cahill
    b) Marty Morrissey
    c) Brian Carthy

20. *All in my head* is the biography of which intercounty hurler?
    a) DJ Carey
    b) Lar Corbett
    c) Seán Óg Ó hAilpín

Answers to Quiz 28: Club Scene

1. Rathnew
2. Laune Rangers
3. Moyle Rovers
4. Gowna
5. St. Oliver Plunketts and Eoghan Ruadh
6. Skryne
7. Walsh Island
8. Round Towers
9. Nemo Rangers
10. Swatragh
11. Ballina Stephenites
12. Na Rossa
13. Castleblayney Faughs
14. Killeavy
15. Garrycastle
16. Loughlinisland
17. Kilanerin
18. An Cheathrú Rua
19. Errigal Ciarán
20. Michael Glavey's

Quiz 30: 2010s Football

EASY

1. Can you name the Dublin player who scored the winning point in the 2011 All-Ireland Football Final?

2. Which county did Cork beat in the 2010 All-Ireland Final?

3. Whom did Jim McGuinness succeed as Donegal manager in 2010?

4. In which year was the black card brought into Gaelic Football?

5. Which county won a four-in-a-row of Ulster Under-21 Football Championships in 2011, 2012, 2013, and 2014?

6. Can you name the brothers who both won the All-Stars Footballer of the Year Award in the 2010s?

7. Which team appeared in its provincial final for the first time ever in 2013?

8. Can you name the player who captained Mayo in the 2012 All-Ireland Final?

9. Who scored 10 points for Roscommon in the 2010 Connacht Final against Sligo?

10. Which county did John Brennan manage in a provincial final during the 2010s?

11. Which county won the Ulster Championship in 2013 for the first time since 1988?

12. Which county won the 2011 All-Ireland Minor Championship for the first time since 1934?

13. Who in 2010 became the first Antrim team to win the All-Ireland Club Championship?

14. Who was the Cork goalkeeper in the 2010 All-Ireland Final?

15. Can you name the Donegal player who was awarded RTÉ Man of the Match after the 2012 All-Ireland Final?

16. Can you name the referee who took charge of the 2010 Leinster Final between Louth and Meath?

17. Which county did Kerry defeat in the 2013 All-Ireland Quarter-Final?

18. Which county did Mick O'Dwyer take charge of in 2012?

19. In which year did Mícheál Ó Muircheartaigh commentate on his last All-Ireland Final?
    a) 2010
    b) 2011
    c) 2012

20. Who managed Dublin to the 2011 All-Ireland?
    a) Paul Caffrey
    b) Pat Gilroy
    c) Jim Gavin

Answers to Quiz 29: GAA Books

1. Fr. Tommy Maher
2. Jim Stynes
3. Brendan Fullam
4. Billy Morgan
5. Sportsfile
6. St. Joseph's Doora-Barefield
7. Desmond Fahy
8. 1990s
9. Moss Keane
10. Waterford
11. Stockholm
12. *Come What May*
13. Mícheál Ó Muircheartaigh
14. Mayo
15. Liam Hayes
16. 1982
17. Dick Fitzgerald
18. Joe Lennon
19. c) Brian Carthy
20. b) Lar Corbett

Quiz 31: 2010s Hurling

1. Who captained Tipperary to the All-Ireland title in 2010?

2. Can you name the Galway club that won the 2013 All-Ireland Club Championship with five Burke brothers on the panel?

3. Which player won the All-Stars Young Hurler of the Year Award in 2012?

4. Can you name the goalkeeper who won All-Star Awards in 2012 and 2013?

5. Which county did Dublin beat in the 2011 National Hurling League Final?

6. Who captained Clare to All-Ireland Hurling success in 2013?

7. In which year did Antrim appear in the All-Ireland Under-21 Final for the first time?

8. How many goals did Lar Corbett score in the 2010 All-Ireland Final?

9. Which county appeared in its first provincial final since 1946 in 2011?

10. Who was the Clare manager during the 2011 Hurling Championship?

11. Can you name the Waterford player who scored a late goal in the 2010 Munster Final Replay?

12. Who won the 2012 Christy Ring Cup Final against Wicklow?

13. Prior to 2013, when did Clare last appear in an All-Ireland Hurling Final?

14. Can you name the Kilkenny player who finished top scorer with 3–56 in the 2012 All-Ireland Senior Championship?

15. How many goals did Cork score against Laois in their All-Ireland Qualifier match in 2011?

16. Can you name the four-time Galway All-Star who retired from intercounty hurling at the end of the 2010 season?

17. Who captained Wexford to the Leinster Under-21 Championship in 2013?

18. Who scored Clare's fifth goal in the 2013 All-Ireland Final Replay?

19. By how many points did Galway beat Kilkenny in the 2012 Leinster Final?
    a) 8
    b) 10
    c) 12

20. Which county did Tipperary beat in the All-Ireland Minor Final in 2012?
    a) Galway
    b) Kilkenny
    c) Dublin

Answers to Quiz 30: 2010s Football

1. Stephen Cluxton
2. Down
3. John Joe Doherty
4. 2014
5. Cavan
6. Alan and Bernard Brogan
7. London
8. David Clarke
9. Donal Shine
10. Derry
11. Monaghan
12. Tipperary
13. St. Gall's
14. Alan Quirke
15. Michael Murphy
16. Martin Sludden
17. Cavan
18. Clare
19. a) 2010
20. b) Pat Gilroy

Quiz 32: Club Scene

EASY

In which county would you find the following clubs?

1. Carnew Emmets

2. Killoe

3. Doohamlet O'Neills

4. St. Jude's

5. Lissycasey

6. Shrule/Glencorrib

7. Bryansford

8. Four Masters

9. O'Dempseys

10. Slaughtneil

11. Shelmaliers

12. Boardsmill

13. Tracton

14. Skeheenarinky

15. Four Roads

16. Railyard

17. Castletown-Finea-Coole-Whitehall

18. Coa

19. Drumcliffe/Rosses Point

20. Tynagh-Abbey/Duniry

Answers to Quiz 31: 2010s Hurling

1. Eoin Kelly
2. St. Thomas'
3. Johnny Coen
4. Anthony Nash
5. Kilkenny
6. Patrick Donnellan
7. 2013
8. Three
9. Armagh
10. Ger O'Loughlin
11. Dan Shanahan
12. London
13. 2002
14. Henry Shefflin
15. Ten
16. Ollie Canning
17. Lee Chin
18. Darach Honan
19. b) 10
20. c) Dublin

Quiz 33: Sponsors

Which county have each of these companies sponsored?

1. Bushmills

2. Harte Peat

3. O_2

4. Mahon and McPhilips

5. Supermacs

6. Clifford Electrical

7. Hilamar Hotel

8. The Bush Hotel

9. Kepak

10. Ladbrokes

11. Tayto Park

12. Tegral

13. Barry's Tea

14. Finches

15. Arnotts

16. Carroll Meats

17. Tracey Concrete

18. Gain Feeds

19. Magee Tailored

20. Meadow Meats

Answers to Quiz 32: Club Scene

1. Wicklow
2. Longford
3. Monaghan
4. Dublin
5. Clare
6. Mayo
7. Down
8. Donegal
9. Laois
10. Derry

11. Wexford
12. Meath
13. Cork
14. Tipperary
15. Roscommon
16. Kilkenny
17. Westmeath
18. Fermanagh
19. Sligo
20. Galway

Medium Quizzes

Quiz 34: Cups

MEDIUM

1. Which county was the first winner of the Liam MacCarthy Cup?

2. The winners of the All-Ireland Senior Ladies' Football Championship are presented with which cup?

3. In which year was the Sam Maguire Cup first presented to the winners of the All-Ireland Senior Football Championship?

4. The Ulster Senior Football Championship cup shares its name with which newspaper?

5. Who was the first captain to be presented with the new Sam Maguire Cup?

6. Which province does not have a name for its Senior Football Championship cup?

7. The Leinster Senior Football Championship cup is named after the Delaney brothers. For which county did they play?

8. The winners of which senior provincial championship are awarded the Bob O'Keeffe Cup?

9. Which cup is presented to the winners of the All-Ireland Minor Hurling Championship?

10. The Sam Maguire Cup is modelled on which famous Early Christian chalice?

11. The All-Ireland fourth-tier hurling championship cup is named after Lory Meagher. For which county did Lory play?

12. The Leinster and Ulster Minor Football Championship cups are named after the same man. Who is he?

13. The winners of the Connacht Senior Football Championship are presented with which cup?

14. Former Taoiseach Charles J Haughey has a GAA cup named after him for which sport?

15. The Cross of Cashel Cup is presented to the winners of which competition?

16. Which former intercounty manager compiled the 2013 book *GAA Family Silver* about the 101 cups and trophies of the GAA?

17. The MacRory Cup is presented to the winners of which competition?

18. Which cup is presented to the winners of the annual Munster hurling competition played in January and February?

19. What is the name of the cup presented to the winners of the All-Ireland Senior Camogie Championship?
a) O'Byrne Cup
b) Ó Fiach Cup
c) O'Duffy Cup

20. The Dr. Croke Cup is presented to the winners of which competition?
a) National Hurling League
b) Munster Senior Hurling Championship
c) Under-21 All-Ireland Championship?

MEDIUM

Answers to Quiz 66: In Which Year?

1.	1994	11.	1968
2.	1951	12.	1971
3.	1961	13.	1981
4.	1947	14.	2010
5.	1958	15.	1981
6.	1987	16.	1998
7.	1999	17.	1991
8.	2007	18.	2010
9.	1974	19.	b) 1989
10.	1941	20.	c) 1977

Quiz 35: Politics

1. With which Cork football team did Jack Lynch win two Cork Senior Football Championships?

2. Which former Kerry All-Ireland-winning captain contested the 1981 general election as an independent candidate?

3. Can you name the former government minister who became the youngest ever Tipperary County Board chairman?

4. Who is the only All-Ireland Senior Football Captain to have lifted the Sam Maguire Cup and later been elected as a Labour Party TD?

5. Can you name the TD who was elected to the Dáil Éireann while he was an intercounty manager during the 2000s?

6. For which party did former Dublin player John O'Leary run in the 2007 general election?

7. Which former All-Ireland winner resigned his Dáil seat in 1970 in protest against his party leader Jack Lynch's policy on Northern Ireland?

8. For which political party did Barney Rock contest the 1991 local elections?

9. Which current Sinn Féin TD won an All-Ireland Under-21 Football Championship?

10. Can you name the All-Ireland-winning captain who was a Dáil deputy when he lifted the Sam Maguire Cup?

11. Can you name the former Westminster MP who played senior football for Armagh during the 1950s?

12. With which club did Charlie Haughey win a Dublin Senior Football Championship in 1945?

13. Name the Ulster Unionist leader who controversially said in 2010 that he would not attend GAA matches.

14. Which party did Seán Kelly represent when he won a European Parliament seat in 2009?

15. The son of which current political party leader played championship football during the 2000s?

16. Can you name the former Ceann Comhairle who played intercounty football during the 1960s?

17. Both parents of which Ulster All-Ireland winner from the 1990s were Sinn Féin councillors?

18. Can you name the Dáil minister, who died during the Civil War, who played for Dublin in an All-Ireland Final and later served as chairman of the county board?

19. How many All-Ireland medals did current TD Jimmy Deenihan win as a player?
    a) 5   b) 6   c) 7

20. Former MEP and TD Mark Clinton played in an All-Ireland Senior Football Final for which county?
    a) Offaly   b) Westmeath   c) Meath

MEDIUM

Answers to Quiz 34: Cups

1. Limerick (1921)
2. The Brendan Martin Cup
3. 1928
4. The Anglo-Celt
5. Joe Cassells (Meath)
6. Munster
7. Laois
8. Leinster hurling
9. The Irish Press Cup
10. The Ardagh Chalice
11. Kilkenny
12. Fr. Larry Murray
13. JJ Nestor Cup
14. Rounders
15. Under-21 hurling
16. Humphrey Kelleher
17. Ulster football colleges
18. The Waterford Crystal Cup
19. c) O'Duffy Cup
20. a) National Hurling League

Quiz 36: Underdogs

1. Who managed Westmeath to its first ever Leinster Senior Football Championship?

2. Which county won its first provincial hurling championship in over ninety years during the 2000s?

3. Which division-four team knocked Mayo out of the 2010 All-Ireland Championship?

4. Who captained Antrim in the 1989 All-Ireland Hurling Final?

5. Which county did the Underdogs play in the first series of TG4's *The Underdogs*?

6. Who knocked All-Ireland champions Armagh out of the 2003 Ulster Championship?

7. In which year did Sligo upset the odds by defeating Mayo in a Connacht Final replay?

8. Who captained Offaly to All-Ireland success in 1982?

9. Which county appeared in its provincial final for the first time in 29 years in 2009?

10. Name the Monaghan club that lost the 1979 All-Ireland Club Football Championship.

11. Which county won the 2006 All-Ireland Minor Football Championship?

12. Which two counties did London beat in the 2013 Connacht Championship?

13. Which county did Limerick beat in the 2007 All-Ireland Hurling Semi-Final?

14. Can you name the Footballer of the Year who played for the Underdogs in TG4's *The Underdogs* before making his intercounty debut?

15. Who scored Clare's only goal in the 1995 Munster Senior Hurling Final?

16. Up to 2013, how many All-Ireland Finals has Mayo lost since it last won in 1951?

17. Which county won its only provincial title in 1944?

18. In which year did Mick O'Dwyer manage Laois to a Leinster Championship?

19. Apart from Cork and Kerry, which is the only other county to win a Munster Senior Football Championship since 1950?
    a) Clare
    b) Tipperary
    c) Limerick

20. What odds were Armagh to win the 2002 All-Ireland Championship before it began?
    a) 8/1
    b) 11/1
    c) 14/1

Answers to Quiz 35: Politics

1. St. Nicholas'
2. Mick O'Connell
3. Michael Lowry
4. Dan Spring
5. Tony Dempsey
6. Fianna Fáil
7. Des Foley
8. Progressive Democrats
9. Martin Ferris
10. Seán Flanagan
11. Seamus Mallon
12. Parnells
13. Tom Elliott
14. Fine Gael
15. Gerry Adams
16. Séamus Kirk
17. Joe Brolly
18. Harry Boland
19. a) 5
20. c) Meath

MEDIUM

Quiz 37: Important Scores

1. Who scored Dublin's only goal in the 2011 All-Ireland Football Final?

2. Can you name the Galway hurler who scored three goals against Kilkenny in the 2005 All-Ireland Hurling Semi-Final?

3. Can you name the Meath player who scored the late goal against Dublin in the third replay of its Leinster Championship match in 1991?

4. Gerry Lohan sealed victory with a late goal in a provincial final for which county during the 2000s?

5. Can you name the Galway player who scored his side's only goal in both the 1987 and 1988 All-Ireland Hurling Finals?

6. Aidan Fogarty scored 1–3 for Kilkenny in the All-Ireland Final of which year?

7. Who eventually scored the point for Galway in the 1998 All-Ireland Final, in a move that came from Michael Donnellan's famous run?

8. Who scored Clare's final point in the 1997 All-Ireland Senior Hurling Final?

9. Can you name the Clare defender who scored the equalizing point in the drawn 2013 All-Ireland Hurling Final?

10. Which Kerry goalkeeper did Séamus Darby score a goal against in the 1982 All-Ireland Football Final?

11. Can you name the Meath player who scored the equalizing goal against Westmeath in the 2001 All-Ireland Quarter-Final?

12. Can you name the Armagh player who missed a penalty and later scored a goal in the 2002 All-Ireland Football Final?

13. Who scored Galway's only goal in an All-Ireland Finals of 1964, 1965, and 1966?

14. Name the Mayo player who scored the winning point against Dublin in the 2006 All-Ireland Football Semi-Final.

15. Who scored Cork's late goal in the 1983 Munster Football Final against Kerry?

16. Who scored Wexford's late goal against Kilkenny in the 2004 Leinster Senior Hurling Semi-Final?

17. Who scored Kerry's only goal in the 1981 All-Ireland Football Final?

18. Can you name the Cork player who scored two goals in the 1986 All-Ireland Hurling Final?

19. Who scored Tyrone's only goal in the 2008 All-Ireland Final?
    a) Tommy McGuigan   b) Seán Cavanagh   c) Martin Penrose

20. Which of these Tipperary players did not score a goal in the 2010 All-Ireland Hurling Final?
    a) Noel McGrath   b) Eoin Kelly   c) Lar Corbett

MEDIUM

Answers to Quiz 36: Underdogs

1. Páidí Ó Sé
2. Derry
3. Longford
4. Ciarán Barr
5. Dublin
6. Monaghan
7. 1975
8. Richie Connor
9. Antrim
10. Scotstown
11. Roscommon
12. Sligo and Leitrim
13. Waterford
14. Kieran Donaghy
15. Davy Fitzgerald
16. Seven
17. Carlow
18. 2003
19. a) Clare
20. c) 14/1

Quiz 38: Family Ties

1. Can you name the three sets of Offaly brothers to have won All-Star Awards?

2. Can you name the Donegal brothers who both started the 2012 All-Ireland Final?

3. Can you name the twin brothers who won All-Ireland medals during the 2000s?

4. Can you name the former All-Star who is grandson to both former GAA President Séamus Ó Riain and former GAA Director General Seán Ó Suíocháin?

5. Can you name the Dublin siblings who won All-Ireland Championships in 2010 and 2011?

6. The Tavey brothers John and Paddy marked each other in a championship match playing for which counties?

7. Can you name the brothers who won All-Star Awards in different codes while representing different counties?

8. The son of Offaly All-Ireland winner Tomás Connor currently plays intercounty football for which county?

9. With which Cork club are the Ó hAilpín brothers associated?

10. Can you name the Derry brothers who have both won All-Star Awards?

11. The father of Dublin All-Ireland winner Paul Curran won an All-Ireland medal with which county?

12. Can you name the Dublin brothers who have both won the All-Stars Footballer of the Year Award?

13. The son of former Dublin All-Ireland winner Des Ferguson won All-Ireland medals with which county?

14. Can you name the Clare brothers who have both won All-Star Awards?

15. With which county did Rhona O'Mahony, daughter of former Leitrim, Galway, and Mayo manager John O'Mahony, play for in an All-Ireland Ladies' Football Final?

16. Paddy Lyons, father of All-Ireland-winning captain Mick, played football for which county?

17. Camogie Team of the Century full-back Marie Costine is the aunt of which former Cork hurler?

18. Can you name the Tyrone brothers who started the 2008 All-Ireland Football Final?

19. How many of the seven Kilkenny Fennelly brothers went on to captain the Kilkenny Senior Hurling Team?
    a) 3   b) 4   c) 5

20. Which of the Ó Sé brothers did not win the All-Stars Footballer of the Year Award?
    a) Darragh   b) Tomás   c) Marc

MEDIUM

Answers to Quiz 37: Important Scores

1. Kevin McManamon
2. Niall Healy
3. Kevin Foley
4. Roscommon
5. Noel Lane
6. 2006
7. Seán Óg de Paor
8. Jamesie O'Connor
9. Domhnall O'Donovan
10. Charlie Nelligan
11. Ollie Murphy
12. Oisín McConville
13. Mattie McDonagh
14. Ciarán McDonald
15. Tadhg Murphy
16. Michael Jacob
17. Jack O'Shea
18. Kevin Hennessy
19. a) Tommy McGuigan
20. b) Eoin Kelly

Quiz 39: Who Said That?

Identify the person reponsible for each of these quotations:

1. 'We were like startled earwigs.'

2. 'I love football, I don't just like it. You can't just like it.'

3. 'In football, it is the winning combination that counts. The same applies to dosing cattle.'

4. 'If Offaly win the National League again this year, it will be the greatest accident since the *Titanic*.'

5. '1–5 to 0–8, well from Lapland to the Antarctic, that's level scores in any man's language.'

6. 'You get more contact in an old-time waltz at the old-folks' home than in a National League Final.'

7. 'It's the memories of matches and fellas you played with that you'll bring to your grave.'

8. 'I don't want to see you coming back in here with dirty jerseys, I want to see ye with blood-stained jerseys, so get out now boys and enjoy yourselves.'

9. 'Whenever a team loses, there's a row at half-time, but when they win, it's an inspirational speech.'

10. 'Play every match as if it was your last, but play well enough to ensure it isn't.'

11. 'Hurling is the bane of my life.'

12. 'GAA executives should accept the validity of the Gaelic Players' Association and abandon the old bloody nonsense of burying their heads in the sand.'

13. 'While there were claims that managers were being paid under the table, the GAA couldn't even find the table.'

14. 'The All-Ireland Championship ruins your life.'

15. 'Sometimes, I'll look at the lads and I'll know what I planned for them is all wrong. I'll just tear it up in my head and start again.'

16. 'Liam Griffin had built us up so much, we thought we could fly.'

17. 'I think of myself as a socialist hurler. I'm not too bothered with the scores as long as I win.'

18. 'In my day, we had a few farmers, a few fishermen, and a college boy to take the frees.'

19. 'Hurling and sex are the only things you can enjoy without being good at.'

20. 'The GAA aren't sharing their revenue with us; why should we have to share ours with them?'

Answers to Quiz 38: Family Ties

1. Lowrys, Connors, and Connors
2. Neil and Éamon McGee
3. John and Tony McEntee
4. Shane Ryan
5. Stephen and Avril Cluxton
6. Monaghan and Cavan
7. Tommy and Declan Carr
8. Kildare
9. Na Piarsaigh
10. Anthony and John McGurk
11. Meath
12. Bernard and Alan Brogan
13. Meath
14. Brian and Frank Lohan
15. Armagh
16. Kildare
17. Donal Óg Cusack
18. Justin and Joe McMahon
19. b) 4
20. a) Darragh

MEDIUM

Quiz 40: Dual Codes

1. With which county did Ireland rugby international Rob Kearney play minor football?

2. With which London soccer club did Kerry footballer Darran O'Sullivan play under-age soccer?

3. Current Carlton Australian Rules footballer Ciarán Sheehan won an All-Ireland medal with which county?

4. Niall Griffin, son of former Wexford manager Liam, competed in the 2004 and 2008 Olympic Games in which sport?

5. In which year did Mick Galwey win his only All-Ireland medal with Kerry?

6. For which soccer club does David Meyler, son of intercounty hurling manager John, play?

7. Can you name the Dublin footballer who won an FA Youth Cup with Ipswich Town in 2005?

8. With which county was Olympic canoeist Eoin Rheinisch involved in training in 2009?

9. With which Dublin GAA club did former rugby international Brian O'Driscoll play in his youth?

10. Current League of Ireland goalkeeper Michael Schlingermann played in an All-Ireland Minor Football Final during the 2000s for which county?

11. The daughter of which former midland intercounty manager currently plays rugby for Ireland?

12. In which year did Niall Quinn play in an All-Ireland Minor Hurling Final?

13. Which current Cork hurler signed for Nottingham Forest when he was sixteen?

14. Who was the first Irishman and former footballer to win the Brownlow Medal during his Australian Rules career?

15. Can you name the Paralympic medallist who lined out for his county in the 2001 Leinster Under-21 Football Championship?

16. During the 1990s, a set of brothers had a player on the Ireland rugby team and their native county hurling team. Who were they?

17. Can you name the midfielder who played in an All-Ireland Final and who has also participated in international mixed martial arts competitions?

18. Can you name the former Ireland rugby international who won a Dublin Under-21 Football Championship in 1995?

19. In which year did the GAA abolish 'Rule 27', the ban on members from attending and playing foreign games?
a) 1951   b) 1961   c) 1971

20. Which county did Ireland rugby player Tomás O'Leary captain to All-Ireland Minor Hurling Championship success?
a) Galway   b) Cork   c) Limerick

MEDIUM

Answers to Quiz 39: Who Said That?

1. Pat Gilroy
2. John Maughan
3. Mick O'Connell
4. Paul O'Kelly
5. Micheál Ó Muircheartaigh
6. Pat Spillane
7. Donal Óg Cusack
8. Jon Kenny (*D'Unbelievables*)
9. John O'Mahony
10. Jack Lynch
11. Ger Loughnane
12. Mick O'Dwyer
13. Peter Quinn
14. Liam McHale
15. Seán Boylan
16. Martin Storey
17. Cormac Bonner
18. Paddy Bawn Brosnan
19. Joe Deane
20. Brian Corcoran

Quiz 41: Transfers

1. Former Galway All-Ireland winner John Divilly later played for which county?

2. For how many counties did Westmeath native PJ Ward play?

3. Can you name the Kerry native who won an All-Star while playing for a different county during the 1990s?

4. Armagh All-Ireland winners Kieran McGeeney, Enda McNulty, and Justin McNulty played together for which Dublin club?

5. In which year did Mayo native Billy Joe Padden make his Armagh debut?

6. Can you name the player who won five Connacht Senior Championships with Galway during the 1980s and two with Mayo in the 1990s?

7. Who was the one Tipperary man who played for Dublin against his native county in the 1961 All-Ireland Final?

8. To which county did Offaly All-Ireland winner Seán Lowry transfer to during the 1980s?

9. For which three counties has Austin O'Malley played in the Senior Football Championship?

10. Former Kilkenny captain Denis Byrne finished his intercounty career with which county?

11. With which two counties did Martin Carney win provincial medals?

12. From which town were three out of the four midfielders who started the 1942 All-Ireland Football Final between Dublin and Galway?

13. To which county did Kerry native Billy Sheehan transfer in 2004?

14. Can you name the player who won a Leinster Club Championship in 2003 and an Ulster Club Championship in 2009?

15. Can you name the Kilkenny native who played against his native county in an All-Ireland Final during the 1970s?

16. To which Dublin club did Éamonn Fennell controversially transfer in 2011?

17. Can you name the player who won a Leinster Under-21 Football Championship and a Munster Senior Football Championship during the 1980s?

18. Dublin All-Ireland winner Vinnie Murphy played hurling for which county during the 1990s?

19. In which year did Dublin native Declan Darcy captain Leitrim to Connacht success?
    a) 1990   b) 1992   c) 1994

20. To which county did former Kildare footballer James Kavanagh transfer in late 2013?
    a) Limerick   b) Galway   c) Sligo

MEDIUM

Answers to Quiz 40: Dual Codes

1. Louth	11. Bobby Miller
2. Queen's Park Rangers	12. 1983
3. Cork	13. Cathal Naughton
4. Equestrianism	14. Jim Stynes
5. 1986	15. Mark Rohan
6. Hull City	16. Brian and Niall Rigney
7. Shane Supple	17. Kalum King
8. Westmeath	18. Eric Miller
9. Clontarf	19. c) 1971
10. Mayo	20. b) Cork

Quiz 42: Under-21 Hurling

1. Which county completed a three-in-a-row of All-Ireland Under-21 Championships from 2000 to 2002?

2. Who captained Waterford to All-Ireland Under-21 success in 1992?

3. How many All-Ireland-winning Under-21 captains from the 2000s have gone on to lift the Liam MacCarthy Cup as All-Ireland-winning senior captain?

4. Can you name the Galway forward who scored two goals in the 2007 All-Ireland Under-21 Final?

5. Who managed Galway to All-Ireland Under-21 success in 2011?

6. Can you name the Dublin player who was top scorer in the 2011 Under-21 Championship?

7. In which year did Cork last appear in an All-Ireland Under-21 Final?

8. Which county did Clare beat in the 2013 Under-21 All-Ireland Final?

9. Who is the only player to have won four Munster Under-21 Championships on the field of play?

10. Who were the first winners of the All-Ireland Under-21 Hurling Championship in 1964?

11. Who sponsored the Under-21 Hurling Championship from 2003 to 2007?

12. By which county and in which year was the double of All-Ireland Under-21 Hurling and Football Championships last achieved?

13. Which former All-Star hurler managed the Carlow Under-21 team in 2011 and 2012?

14. Who managed Clare to All-Ireland Under-21 success in 2009?

15. Cork beat which county after a second replay to win the 1966 Under-21 All-Ireland Championship?

16. In which year did Wexford win its only Under-21 All-Ireland?

17. True or false: Dublin has never won an Under-21 All-Ireland Championship?

18. Jack Ryan, father of Dublin dual player Shane, won an All-Ireland Under-21 Championship with which county?

19. Which of the following players never won an Under-21 All-Ireland Championship?
    a) Noel McGrath
    b) Diarmuid O'Sullivan
    c) Walter Walsh

20. How many times has Kilkenny completed a treble of Senior, Under-21, and Minor All-Ireland titles?
    a) 3
    b) 4
    c) 5

MEDIUM

Answers to Quiz 41: Transfers

1. Kildare
2. Three
3. Karl O'Dwyer
4. Na Fianna
5. 2011
6. Tomás Tierney
7. Paddy Croke
8. Mayo
9. Mayo, Dublin, and Wicklow
10. Tipperary
11. Donegal and Mayo
12. Dingle
13. Laois
14. Rory Gallagher
15. Matt Ruth
16. St. Vincent's
17. Larry Tompkins
18. Kerry
19. c) 1994
20. b) Galway

Quiz 43: Under-21 Football

1. Which county won a three-in-a-row of All-Ireland Under-21 titles during the 1980s?

2. Who captained Tyrone to All-Ireland Under-21 titles in 1991 and 1992?

3. Who won its first Under-21 All-Ireland in 1999?

4. Which is the only Munster county not to have won the Munster Under-21 Football Championship?

5. Which county won All-Ireland Under-21 Championships in 1982 and 1987?

6. Who managed Dublin to two All-Ireland Under-21 Championships during the 2010s?

7. In which year did Kerry win the treble of Senior, Under-21, and Minor All-Irelands?

8. True or false: Longford has never won a Leinster Under-21 Championship?

9. Can you name the two Galway forwards who scored three goals each in the 2005 All-Ireland Final?

10. Which county won its first Under-21 provincial title in 2011?

11. Which county won four Ulster Under-21 titles in a row during the 2010s?

12. Can you name the Cork player who won the Cadbury Hero of the Future Award in 2009?

13. Which was the first Ulster county to win the Under-21 All-Ireland Championship?

14. Which county did Tyrone beat in the 2000 Under-21 All-Ireland Final?

15. Can you name the only Galway player to start both the 2011 and the 2013 All-Ireland Under-21 Finals?

16. Can you name the only Connacht county not to have won the Connacht Under-21 Football Championship?

17. Which was the last county to complete a double of Senior and Under-21 Football Championships?

18. Who captained Dublin to All-Ireland success in 2003?

19. How many Kerry players started both the 1973 All-Ireland Under-21 Final and the 1975 All-Ireland Senior Final?
    a) 9   b) 10   c) 11

20. Which of these counties has appeared in an All-Ireland Under-21 Final?
    a) Leitrim
    b) Monaghan
    c) Fermanagh

MEDIUM

Answers to Quiz 42: Under-21 Hurling

1. Limerick
2. Tony Browne
3. Three
4. Conor Kavanagh
5. Anthony Cunningham
6. Kevin O'Loughlin
7. 1998
8. Antrim
9. Mick Malone
10. Tipperary

11. Erin Foods
12. Galway in 2011
13. Paul Flynn
14. John Minogue
15. Wexford
16. 1965
17. True
18. Tipperary
19. c) Walter Walsh
20. a) 3

Quiz 44: Early Years

1. Mick Gill won All-Ireland medals with which two counties in the 1920s?

2. How many Ulster titles did Cavan win during the 1930s?

3. In which year did Dublin last win the All-Ireland Senior Hurling Championship?

4. What name is given to the 1939 All-Ireland Hurling Final?

5. In which room of Hayes' Hotel was the GAA established?

6. Which county won its only All-Ireland Hurling Championship in 1901?

7. In which year was the Camogie Association founded?

8. Which county did Cork beat by 27 points in the 1943 All-Ireland Hurling Final?

9. Where was the first ever All-Ireland Football Final played?

10. Who was the first President of the GAA?

11. Where was the 1937 All-Ireland Hurling Final between Tipperary and Kilkenny played?

12. Which was the first county to be presented with the Sam Maguire Cup in 1928?

13. Michael Hogan was playing for which county when he was shot on Bloody Sunday in 1920?

14. Who was the first player to be sent off in an All-Ireland Football Final?

15. Which non-Dublin-based club won an All-Ireland representing Dublin in 1902?

16. Which county won a four-in-a-row of All-Ireland Football Championships during the 1910s?

17. GAA General Secretary from 1901 to 1929 Luke O'Toole was a native of which county?

18. Which county made its only appearance in an All-Ireland Football Final in 1930?

19. Which county won the inaugural Senior Hurling Championship?
    a) Tipperary
    b) Cork
    c) Dublin

20. How many All-Ireland Football Championships had Dublin won before Kerry won its first one?
    a) 6
    b) 8
    c) 10

Answers to Quiz 43: Under-21 Football

1. Cork
2. Peter Canavan
3. Westmeath
4. Clare
5. Donegal
6. Jim Gavin
7. 1975
8. True
9. Seán Armstrong and Michael Meehan
10. Wexford
11. Cavan
12. Colm O'Neill
13. Derry (1968)
14. Limerick
15. Fiontán Ó Curraoin
16. Sligo
17. Cork (1989)
18. Alan Brogan
19. a) 9
20. c) Fermanagh

Quiz 45: Croke Park

MEDIUM

1. In which year did the GAA buy Croke Park?

2. Whom did the English RFU get to talk to their players about the history of Croke Park before their game in 2007?

3. Which Dublin soccer club used Croke Park until the GAA purchased the area?

4. How many corporate boxes are there in Croke Park?

5. Can you name the American musician who sold out five nights in Croke Park in 2014?

6. Who scored the first rugby try in Croke Park?

7. In which year was the first floodlit game played in Croke Park?

8. After whom is the media area in the Hogan Stand named?

9. Can you name the French soccer player who scored the only goal against Ireland during their 2009 World Cup play-off at Croke Park?

10. Whom did Muhammed Ali fight in Croke Park in 1972?

11. What was the Canal End renamed in 2007?

12. The rubble from which Dublin street was used to make Hill 16?

13. True or false: a baseball exhibition game was played in Croke Park in 1946?

14. The highest ever attendance in Croke Park was recorded at the All-Ireland Football Final in which year?

15. What is the official name of the walkway that stands above Croke Park?

Answers – page 95

16. Who was the first All-Ireland Hurling winning captain to be presented with the Liam MacCarthy Cup on the centre of the field in Croke Park?

17. Where was the original Nally Stand from Croke Park later re-erected?

18. What was the first stand built in Croke Park?

19. Which of these European stadiums has a smaller capacity than Croke Park?
    a) Stade de France
    b) Wembley Stadium
    c) Camp Nou

20. How many acres does the total area of Croke Park cover?
    a) 8
    b) 12
    c) 16

MEDIUM

Answers to Quiz 44: Early Years

1. Galway and Dublin
2. Eight
3. 1938
4. The Thunder and Lightning Final
5. The Billiard Room
6. London
7. 1904
8. Antrim
9. Clonskeagh, Dublin
10. Maurice Davin

11. Fitzgerald Stadium, Killarney
12. Kildare
13. Tipperary
14. Joe Stafford (1943)
15. Bray Emmets
16. Wexford
17. Wicklow
18. Monaghan
19. a) Tipperary
20. b) 8

Quiz 46: GAA Media

1. Who presented live GAA games on TV3 from 2008 to 2013?

2. What is the name of the weekly GAA newspaper based in Omagh, Co. Tyrone?

3. Who succeeded Michael Lyster in presenting the *Sunday Game* highlights programme in 2004?

4. In which year were the All-Ireland Finals broadcast live on television for the first time?

5. The fictional GAA club of Kildoran on RTÉ's *On Home Ground* series played in which county?

6. Former intercounty players Diarmuid Lyng and Colm Parkinson are presenters on which radio station?

7. Liam Cahill founded and edited which former GAA website and discussion forum?

8. What was the name of the official GAA magazine for children that came free with the *Irish Times*?

9. Can you name the former journalist who was Gaelic Games correspondent with the *Irish Times* from 1962 to 1994?

10. Which county did *Irish Independent* journalist Eugene McGee manage to All-Ireland success?

11. Who was the first presenter of the *Sunday Game* in 1979?

12. Which former All-Ireland-winning captain presents *Seó Spóirt* on TG4?

13. How many All-Ireland Finals did Mícheál Ó Hehir commentate on during his career?

14. In which year did Mícheál Ó Muircheartaigh commentate on RTÉ for the first time?

15. Who presented the long running RTÉ radio programme *Gaelic Sports Results* on Sunday nights from 1953 to 2011?

16. Can you name the subscription-based television channel that was established in 1990 to facilitate the broadcasting of Irish sporting events around the world?

17. Which Clare football club did broadcaster Marty Morrissey play for and manage?

18. Which GAA personality has the most Twitter followers?

19. All-Ireland-winning captains Ray Silke and Dara Ó Cinnéide are regular columnists with with newspaper?
    a) *The Irish Star*
    b) *The Irish Times*
    c) *The Irish Examiner*

20. How many All-Ireland Senior medals have *Sunday Game* analysts Pat Spillane, Colm O'Rourke, and Joe Brolly won between them?
    a) 9
    b) 11
    c) 13

MEDIUM

Answers to Quiz 45: Croke Park

1. 1913
2. Conor O'Shea
3. Bohemians FC
4. 87
5. Garth Brooks
6. Raphaël Ibañez
7. 2007
8. Mícheál O'Hehir
9. Nicolas Anelka
10. Al 'Blue' Lewis
11. The Davin Stand
12. O'Connell Street
13. True
14. 1961
15. Etihad Skyline
16. Mark Landers
17. Carrickmore, Co. Tyrone
18. Hogan Stand
19. a) Stade de France
20. c) 16

Quiz 47: All-Stars

1. Can you name the only two counties who have not received an All-Star in either code?

2. Who was Westmeath's first All-Star?

3. Who was the 1000th All-Star Award recipient in 2004?

4. Can you name the Galway player who was the goalkeeper on the first All-Star team in 1971?

5. Who are the only twins to have won All-Star Awards?

6. How many players on the 2013 All-Star Hurling Team won their first award that year?

7. Can you name the only set of Donegal brothers who have won All-Star Awards?

8. Who is the only player to have won both a football and hurling All-Star in the same year?

9. Which was the first county to win an All-Star in every position in both hurling and football?

10. Name the Dublin hurler who won an All-Star Award in 2009.

11. Who is Clare's only football All-Star?

12. Can you name the Tyrone father and son who have both won All-Star Awards?

13. Who was the inaugural winner of the All-Star Footballer of the Year Award in 1995?

14. Name the Limerick hurler who won five consecutive All-Stars during the 1970s.

15. How many All-Star Awards did DJ Carey win during his career?

16. Who is Wicklow's only All-Star?

17. In which year did Henry Shefflin win his first All-Star Award?

18. Can you name the father and son who won All-Stars representing different Connacht counties?

19. Which of these three counties has the most All-Star Awards?
    a) Derry
    b) Kildare
    c) Armagh

20. Which Donegal player was selected as All-Star Footballer of the Year in 2012?
    a) Karl Lacey
    b) Michael Murphy
    c) Colm McFadden

MEDIUM

Answers to Quiz 46: GAA Media

1. Matt Cooper
2. *Gaelic Life*
3. Pat Spillane
4. 1962
5. Kildare
6. Newstalk
7. An Fear Rua
8. *Cúl4Kids*
9. Paddy Downey
10. Offaly
11. Jim Carney
12. Dara Ó Cinnéide
13. 99
14. 1949
15. Seán Óg Ó Ceallacháin
16. Setanta Sports
17. Kilmurry Ibrickane
18. Paul Galvin
19. c) *The Irish Examiner*
20. b) 11

Quiz 48: Club Scene

With which club are these footballers associated?

1. Tony Browne

2. Paul Conroy

3. Neil McManus

4. Paul Finlay

5. Niall McNamee

6. Charlie Harrison

7. Gerard O'Kane

8. Noel McGrath

9. Bryan Cullen

10. Andy Moran

11. Seán Cavanagh

12. Anthony Nash

13. Ciaran McKeever

14. Stephen Bray

15. Brian Hogan

16. Darach Honan

17. Killian Young

18. Ryan McCluskey

19. David Breen

20. Neil Gallagher

Answers to Quiz 47: All-Stars

1. Carlow and Longford
2. David Kilcoyne
3. Paul Galvin
4. PJ Smith
5. Ben and Jerry O'Connor
6. Twelve
7. James and Martin McHugh
8. Ray Cummins
9. Offaly
10. Alan McCrabbe
11. Séamus Clancy
12. Frank and Brian McGuigan
13. Peter Canavan
14. Pat Hartigan
15. Nine
16. Kevin O'Brien
17. 2000
18. Liam and Kevin O'Neill
19. c) Armagh
20. a) Karl Lacey

Quiz 49: Who Said That?

Identify the person responsible for each of these quotations:

1. 'A referee should be like a man. For the most part they are like old women.'

2. 'As for abuse of players or referees. All it does is create an extra layer of noise.'

3. 'Football is a game for those who are not good enough to play hurling.'

4. 'As much won't do. You have to give more every year. That's the way it's gone.'

5. 'Each year I associated the first smell of cut grass with the start of serious football.'

6. 'The most skilful player in the world won't necessarily win a game for you ... The guy who's gonna do the business for you is the one who takes responsibility.'

7. 'Keep close to the goal today, I didn't bring any oxygen.'

8. 'Gaelic Football is personal. It's not a kick around in the park early on a Sunday morning. It's not a run out for the boys.'

9. 'Kerry's brand of catch and kick football is ten years out of date.'

10. 'A No. 3 who fails to assert himself is on his way to being No. 23.'

11. 'You couldn't even begin to imagine the time people like DJ and Henry and JJ spend trying to perfect their skills.'

12. 'Any All-Ireland you beat Kerry in is a double All-Ireland.'

13. 'Anthony Lynch the Cork corner-back will be the last person to let you down ... his people are undertakers.'

14. 'You can't win derbies with donkeys.'

15. 'We wanted to go somewhere they don't know anything about hurling, and it was either Thailand or Tipperary.'

16. 'Meath gloried in intimidating Cork and resorted to fouling to retain their title.'

17. 'There will never be games, believe me, to equal those two games in Thurles in 1940.'

18. 'Hurling is a game of such quick reaction, that even watching a game of football can affect you.'

19. 'Hurling is the *Riverdance* of sport.'

20. 'Our supporters put Dublin posters up beside their Manchester United ones. It was good for the game.'

MEDIUM

Answers to Quiz 48: Club Scene

1. Mount Sion
2. St. James'
3. Ruairí Óg Cushendall
4. Ballybay Pearse Brothers
5. Rhode
6. St. John's
7. John Mitchel's Glenullin
8. Loughmore-Castleiney
9. Skerries Harps
10. Ballaghaderreen
11. Moy
12. Kanturk
13. St. Patrick's
14. Navan O'Mahony's
15. O'Loughlin Gaels
16. Clonlara
17. Renard
18. Enniskillen Gaels
19. Na Piarsaigh
20. Glenswilly

Quiz 50: Minor Football

1. The winners of the All-Ireland Minor Football Championship receive which cup?

2. Which county completed a three-in-a-row of All-Ireland Minor Championships during the 1960s?

3. Which county did Galway beat in the 2007 All-Ireland Minor Final?

4. In which year did Kerry last complete a Minor and Senior All-Ireland double?

5. Who managed Roscommon to All-Ireland minor success in 2006?

6. Ireland rugby international Tommy Bowe played minor football for which county?

7. Who managed Tipperary to All-Ireland Minor Football success in 2011?

8. Which county was the first winner of the All-Ireland Minor Football Championship in 1929?

9. True or false: Kildare has never won an All-Ireland Minor Championship?

10. Which county won its second All-Ireland Minor Football Championship in 2009?

11. Can you name the current Dublin hurler who scored a goal in the 2001 All-Ireland Minor Football Final?

12. Barney Eastwood won All-Ireland Minor Championships in the 1940s with which county?

13. Who captained Armagh to All-Ireland Minor success in 2009?

14. Can you name the actor who celebrated with the Dublin minor football team after its All-Ireland success in 2012?

15. Can you name the Laois player who played in three All-Ireland Minor Finals during the 1990s?

16. In which year did Westmeath win its first All-Ireland Minor Championship?

17. Who was the Mayo All-Ireland-winning Minor manager in 2013?

18. Up to 2013, which is the last county to complete a Minor–Senior double of All-Ireland titles in the same year?

19. How many All-Ireland Minor Finals did Mayo lose during the 2000s?
    a) 3
    b) 4
    c) 5

20. Which one of these Kilkenny hurlers did not play in the Leinster Minor Football Championship in 1997?
    a) Henry Shefflin
    b) Michael Kavanagh
    c) Eddie Brennan

MEDIUM

Answers to Quiz 49: Who Said That?

1.	Billy Rackard	11.	Brian Cody
2.	Donal O'Grady	12.	Kevin Heffernan
3.	Tony Wall	13.	Micheál Ó Muircheartaigh
4.	Pádraic Joyce	14.	Michael 'Babs' Keating
5.	Gay O'Driscoll	15.	Ger Loughnane
6.	Nicky English	16.	Dinny Allen
7.	Billy Morgan	17.	Mick Mackey
8.	Liam Hayes	18.	Justin McCarthy
9.	Joe Lennon	19.	Liam Griffin
10.	Mick Lyons	20.	Jimmy Keaveney

Quiz 51: Minor Hurling

1. Can you name the Waterford player who scored 1–7 in the 2013 All-Ireland Minor Final?

2. Who managed Offaly to three All-Ireland Minor Championships during the 1980s?

3. In which year did Clare win its first All-Ireland Minor Championship?

4. Who captained Kilkenny to All-Ireland Minor success in 1972?

5. For which county did soccer player Shane Long play in the All-Ireland Minor Hurling Championship?

6. Who captained Cork to All-Ireland Minor success in 2001?

7. Who is the only player to captain his county to consecutive All-Ireland Minor Hurling Championships?

8. Who managed Kilkenny to All-Ireland Minor success in 2010?

9. How many All-Ireland Minor Hurling Championships did Limerick win in the fifty years from 1963 to 2013?

10. In which year did Mattie Murphy win his first All-Ireland Minor Championship as Galway manager?

11. Which county was involved in controversy surrounding 'Hawk-Eye' during the 2013 All-Ireland Minor Hurling Championship?

12. Which county scored four goals in an All-Ireland Minor Hurling Final during the 2000s and still lost?

13. In how many All-Ireland Minor Finals did Galway play during the 2000s?

14. Which county did Kilkenny beat in the 2006 Leinster Minor Hurling Final?

15. True or false: no team from Ulster has ever contested an All-Ireland Minor Hurling Final?

16. Up to 2013, in which year was the All-Ireland Minor–Senior double last achieved?

17. In which year did Richie Power captain Kilkenny to All-Ireland Minor success?

18. Can you name the All-Ireland Senior Football Championship winner who scored a goal in an All-Ireland Minor Hurling Final during the 2010s?

19. How many All-Ireland Minor Hurling Championships did Joe Canning win?
    a) 1   b) 2   c) 3

20. Which of these players has not won an All-Ireland Minor Hurling Championship?
    a) DJ Carey   b) Tommy Dunne   c) Joe Deane

MEDIUM

Answers to Quiz 50: Minor Football

1.	Tom Markham Cup	11.	David O'Callaghan
2.	Cork	12.	Tyrone
3.	Derry	13.	Declan McKenna
4.	1980	14.	Daniel Radcliffe
5.	Fergal O'Donnell	15.	Brian McDonald
6.	Monaghan	16.	1995
7.	David Power	17.	Enda Gilvarry
8.	Clare	18.	Tyrone
9.	True	19.	b) 4
10.	Armagh	20.	c) Eddie Brennan

Quiz 52: Occupations

What does each of these GAA players do for a living?

1. Brian Roper

2. Aidan O'Mahony

3. Noel Hickey

4. Michael Carton

5. Brian Dooher

6. Brian Cody

7. Stephen Lucey

8. Donal Óg Cusack

9. Cian Mackey

10. Seán Cavanagh

11. Stephen Molumphy

12. Paul Durcan

13. Joe Brolly

14. Lar Corbett

15. Ryan O'Dwyer

16. Henry Shefflin

17. Conor Gormley

18. Eoin Brosnan

19. Anthony Moyles

20. Charlie Nelligan

MEDIUM

Answers to Quiz 51: Minor Hurling

1. Patrick Curran
2. Pad Joe Whelahan
3. 1997
4. Brian Cody
5. Tipperary
6. Tomás O'Leary
7. Joe Dunphy
8. Richie Mulrooney
9. One
10. 1992

11. Limerick
12. Cork
13. Eight
14. Carlow
15. False
16. 2008
17. 2003
18. Ciarán Kilkenny
19. b) 2
20. b) Tommy Dunne

Quiz 53: Referees and Administrators

1. Can you name the former GAA President who received his All-Ireland medal 55 years after being a substitute on an All-Ireland-winning team?

2. From which county is former General Secretary Liam Mulvihill?

3. In which year did Pat McEnaney referee his first All-Ireland Football Final?

4. Can you name the intercounty referee who played in the 2007 All-Ireland Club Hurling Final?

5. 1983 All-Ireland Football Final referee John Gough is a native of which county?

6. Who was the first General Secretary of the GAA?

7. Can you name the man who refereed an All-Ireland Final in 1953 and won one as a player in 1954?

8. Whom did Liam O'Neill succeed as President of the GAA?

9. Can you name the former GAA President who was elected as an MEP in the 2009 European elections?

10. Who is the only GAA President to be awarded the title of 'Honorary Life President' after he retired?

11. Can you name the former Chairman of the Dublin County Board who ran in the 2002 and 2007 general elections?

12. Who was the last President of the GAA from Dublin?

13. Can you name the major GAA ground that is named after the man who was General Secretary of the GAA from 1929 to 1964?

14. Can you name the Sligo All-Star who later went on to be an intercounty referee?

15. Which referee took charge of the 2013 All-Ireland Football Final?

16. Who was the first Protestant President of the GAA?

17. From which county is intercounty referee Dickie Murphy?

18. In which year did Nickey Brennan become President of the GAA?

19. Which stand in Croke Park is currently named after a former General Secretary of the association?
    a) Cusack Stand
    b) Davin Stand
    c) Dineen Hill 16

20. Former GAA President Seán McCague guided which county to National Football League success?
    a) Roscommon
    b) Monaghan
    c) Laois

MEDIUM

Answers to Quiz 52: Occupations

1. Monumental sculptor
2. Garda
3. Farmer
4. Fireman
5. Veterinarian
6. Primary school teacher
7. Doctor
8. Electrical engineer
9. Plumber
10. Accountant
11. Army
12. Quantity surveyor
13. Barrister
14. Publican
15. Secondary school teacher
16. Bank official
17. Electrician
18. Solicitor
19. Stockbroker
20. Baker

Quiz 54: Teams of the Millennium/Century

1. Who is the only member of the Football Team of the Millennium not to have won an All-Ireland?

2. In which year did Football Team of the Millenium member Mick O'Connell captain Kerry to All-Ireland success?

3. Who is the goalkeeper on the Hurling Team of the Millennium?

4. Who is the only Meath player on the Football Team of the Millennium?

5. Can you name the Wexford hurler who was chosen at full-forward on the Team of the Century, but was not chosen on the Team of the Millennium?

6. Can you name the player who was chosen on the Football Team of the Century of non-All-Ireland-winners, but later went on to win an All-Ireland?

7. Name the Kerry midfielder who was selected on the GAA Team of the Century, but not the Team of the Millennium?

8. How many All-Ireland medals did John Joe O'Reilly, centre-back on both the Football Team of the Century and Millennium, win?

9. Can you name the only player who was still playing to be chosen on the Hurling Team of the Millennium?

10. Can you name the two Kerry players who were managed by Mick O'Dwyer to be selected to the Football Team of the Millennium?

11. With which county did Camogie Team of the Century player Linda Mellerick play?

12. Can you name the two counties who had won All-Ireland Hurling Championships before 1950 not to have any representation on the Team of the Millennium?

13. Who was the only northern player to be selected to the Football Team of the Millennium?

14. Can you name the two players on the Hurling Team of the Millennium who have also won All-Ireland Football medals?

15. Who was the only Waterford player to be selected to the Hurling Team of the Millennium?

16. Can you name the player on the Camogie Team of the Century who won 59 badminton caps for Ireland?

17. Who was the only Dublin footballer chosen on the Football Team of the Millennium?

18. Can you name the Camogie Team of the Century player who boycotted the presentation because her sister was not chosen on the team?

19. Tommy Langan, full-forward on both the Football Team of the Century and Millennium, played for which county?
a) Mayo   b) Kerry   c) Cavan

20. How many Kilkenny hurlers were chosen on the Team of the Millennium?
a) 3   b) 4   c) 5

MEDIUM

Answers to Quiz 53: Referees and Administrators

1. Mick Loftus	11. John Bailey
2. Longford	12. Joseph Stuart
3. 1996	13. Páirc Uí Chaoimh
4. Michael Haverty	14. Mickey Kearins
5. Antrim	15. Joe McQuillan
6. Michael Cusack	16. Jack Boothman
7. Peter McDermott	17. Wexford
8. Christy Cooney	18. 2006
9. Seán Kelly	19. c) Dineen Hill 16
10. James Nowlan	20. b) Monaghan

Quiz 55: Twitter Handles

Identify these GAA personalities by their Twitter handles:

1. @sportsdes

2. @killeavy13

3. @Flinto23

4. @AIDOXI

5. @D_GGs

6. @efitz6

7. @podzo21

8. @polie11

9. @AOMTHECAT

10. @PaddyB14

11. @dsully3

12. @murphm95

13. @townhurler

14. @Begz_17

15. @cads3

16. @conmort

17. @Sohaneytweet

18. @D_Kelloggs

19. @123kav

20. @waggymac

MEDIUM

Answers to Quiz 54: Teams of the Millennium/Century

1. Tommy Murphy
2. 1959
3. Tony Reddin
4. Martin O'Connell
5. Nicky Rackard
6. Dinny Allen
7. Jack O'Shea
8. Two
9. Brian Whelehan
10. Pat Spillane and Mickey Sheehy
11. Cork
12. Galway and Clare
13. Seán O'Neill
14. Jack Lynch and Ray Cummins
15. John Keane
16. Mary Sinnott
17. Kevin Heffernan
18. Angela Downey
19. a) Mayo
20. b) 4

Quiz 56: Who Said That?

Identify the person responsible for each of these quotations:

1. 'Tar éis seacht mblian is caoga, tá craobh na hÉireann ar ais i nGaillimh.'

2. 'The finest players are often sacrificed if they be placed under an incapable leader.'

3. 'I'm always suspicious of games where you're the only ones that play it.'

4. 'In forty minutes I am going across for that cup and I want you all behind me. Here is my speech.'

5. 'If Kerry lose either the manager was to blame or the players were to blame. There's no such thing as you were beaten by the better team.'

6. 'The famine is over.'

7. 'Corner-back can be quite a restrictive position, you don't get much of a chance to do much hurling.'

8. 'The more stitches required after a game in the Cork dressing room, the more probable they had won.'

9. 'In the first half they played with the wind. In the second half they played with the ball.'

10. 'It was intense, but not one Kerry player had to leave that field injured. If anything was injured, it was Kerry's pride.'

11. 'Wicklowmen I knew were experts on atin' cocky corner-forwards without salt.'

12. 'They've suffered these people, they suffered so much over the past years. This is their reward.'

13. 'Clare pissed people off because they didn't conveniently feck off back to Doolin after 1995 and play their music til kingdom come.'

14. 'No comment, and by the way, you can't quote me.'

15. 'A farmer could make a tidy living in the amount of ground it takes Moss Keane to turn.'

16. 'Fermanagh has such a small playing base. Half the county is made up of water and half of the remaining half are Protestants.'

17. 'I often wonder if we changed the names of the counties and jersey colours and started over again, would it make a difference?'

18. 'It amuses me when I hear of teams training first thing in the morning as if it was something brand new. Galway were doing that and more in the 1980s.'

19. 'Every Clare man, woman, and child, came to Cork this weekend on a mission. Our mission was to show that we're no longer the whipping boys of Munster.'

20. 'What we needed was to lose the fear of winning, not the fear of losing.'

Answers to Quiz 55: Twitter Handles

1.	Des Cahill	11.	Diarmuid O'Sullivan
2.	Steven McDonnell	12.	Michael Murphy
3.	Paul Flynn	13.	Shane O'Donnell
4.	Aidan O'Shea	14.	Colm Begley
5.	Daniel Goulding	15.	Eoin Cadogan
6.	Eamonn Fitzmaurice	16.	Conor Mortimer
7.	Padraic Maher	17.	Shane McGrath
8.	Mark Poland	18.	David Kelly
9.	Alan O'Mara	19.	Rory Kavanagh
10.	Paddy Bradley	20.	Wayne McNamara

Quiz 57: Dual Players

1. Can you name the Dublin player who has won five Leinster Senior Football Championships and one Leinster Senior Hurling Championship since 2000?

2. Apart from Cork, which other county has completed a double of All-Ireland Football and Hurling successes in the same year?

3. Who was the Down player who won an Ulster Football Championship in 1991 and an Ulster Hurling Championship in 1992?

4. Which is the only club to have won both the All-Ireland Football and Hurling Club Championship?

5. In which year did a county last compete in the All-Ireland Senior Football and Hurling Finals in the same year?

6. Can you name the Cork dual star who won the 2005 National Female Sportsperson of the Year Award?

7. Can you name the player who won three All-Ireland Senior Hurling Championships with Kilkenny and two All-Ireland Senior Football Championships with Dublin?

8. Can you name the Offaly dual player who has a football and hurling All-Star Award?

9. In 2014, who became the first Connacht player to have won interprovincial championships in both hurling and football?

10. Who won an All-Ireland Football Championship with Derry in 1993 and Ulster Senior Hurling Championship in 2000?

11. In which year did Offaly contest both the All-Ireland Football and Hurling Finals?

12. Who is the only player to have won All-Ireland Football and Hurling Championships at Minor, Under-21, and Senior level in both codes?

13. Can you name the Cavan dual player who has played football for the county and won All-Ireland handball championships?

14. Can you name the Galway player who featured in both the All-Ireland Football and Hurling Finals of 2001?

15. Including replays, which Dublin dual player played in five All-Ireland Minor Finals in the 2010s?

16. Can you name the Cork man who started in and won two All-Ireland Finals in 1990?

17. Who is the only Kildare player to have won Interprovincial medals in both hurling and football?

18. Can you name the 2001 Tipperary All-Ireland Hurling winner who played in the 2002 Munster Football Final?

19. In which year did Cork last appear in both football and hurling All-Ireland Finals?
    a) 1990   b) 1993   c) 1999

20. Between football and hurling, how many All-Ireland Senior Championships did Jack Lynch win as a player?
    a) 4   b) 5   c) 6

MEDIUM

Answers to Quiz 56: Who Said That?

1. Joe Connolly	11. Liam Griffin
2. Dick Fitzgerald	12. Joe Kernan
3. Jack Charlton	13. Anthony Daly
4. Eamonn Grimes	14. Brian Mullins
5. Páidí Ó Sé	15. Danny Lynch
6. Richie Stakelum	16. Des Cahill
7. Frank Lohan	17. Kevin O'Brien
8. Con Murphy	18. Pete Finnerty
9. Micheál Ó Muircheartaigh	19. Anthony Daly
10. Mickey Harte	20. Brian McEniff

Quiz 58: Club Hurling

1. Which cup do the winners of the All-Ireland Club Hurling Championship receive?

2. Four Roads has played in two All-Ireland Semi-Finals. Which county did the club represent?

3. Up to 2014, which is the last Munster club to win the All-Ireland Club Championship?

4. Which was the first Wexford club to win the All-Ireland Club Championship?

5. Can you name the only player who has been presented with the All-Ireland Club Championship Cup on three occasions as winning captain?

6. Which is the only Laois club to have appeared in an All-Ireland Club Hurling Final?

7. John Mullane played in an All-Ireland Club Final with which club during the 2000s?

8. Which is the only Dublin club to have won the Leinster Senior Club Hurling Championship?

9. In which year did Birr win the All-Ireland Club Championship for the first time?

10. Which is the only Ulster club to have won the All-Ireland Club Hurling Championship?

11. Which county leads the way with the most All-Ireland Club Hurling Championships?

12. Eddie Brennan played in an All-Ireland Club Final for which club during the 2000s?

13. Which was the first club from Carlow to contest an All-Ireland Club Championship Final?

14. Which is the only Cork club to have won the All-Ireland Club Championship on three occasions?

15. Which club has won the All-Ireland Club Hurling Championship on five occasions?

16. Up to 2014, how many All-Ireland Club Hurling Championships has Portumna won?

17. Which is the last Leinster club to win back-to-back All-Ireland Club Championships?

18. In which year was the All-Ireland Club Championship first played?

19. Which was the first Clare club to win the All-Ireland Club Championship?
    a) Sixmilebridge
    b) Wolfe Tones
    c) St. Joseph's Doora-Barefield

20. Up to 2014, how many different Galway clubs have won the All-Ireland Club Championship?
    a) 5   b) 6   c) 7

Answers to Quiz 57: Dual Players

1.	Conal Keaney	11.	1981
2.	Tipperary	12.	Brian Murphy
3.	Greg Blaney	13.	Paul Brady
4.	St. Finbarr's	14.	Alan Kerins
5.	2001	15.	Cormac Costello
6.	Briege Corkery	16.	Teddy McCarthy
7.	Pierce Grace	17.	Pat Dunney
8.	Liam Currams	18.	Brendan Cummins
9.	Keith Higgins	19.	c) 1999
10.	Kieran McKeever	20.	c) 6

MEDIUM

Quiz 59: Club Football

1. Clubs from which county have won the All-Ireland Championship on the most occasions?

2. With which club did Pat Spillane win an All-Ireland Club Championship?

3. In which year did Crossmaglen Rangers win the All-Ireland Club Championship for the first time?

4. The winners of the All-Ireland Club Championship receive the Andy Merrigan Cup. Which county was Andy Merrigan from?

5. Who were the first Connacht winners of the All-Ireland Club Championship?

6. Who captained St. Vincent's to All-Ireland success in 2014?

7. Which club has won the All-Ireland Club Championship on seven occasions?

8. Longford attacker Brian Kavanagh won an All-Ireland Club Championship with which club?

9. Which was the first club to win back-to-back All-Ireland Club Championships?

10. Which is the only Meath club to have contested an All-Ireland Club Football Final?

11. Which is the last Kerry club to have won the All-Ireland Club Championship?

12. Former Fermanagh and Cavan player Rory Gallagher won an All-Ireland Club Championship with which club?

13. How many Dublin clubs have won the All-Ireland Club Championship?

14. In which year did Baltinglass win the All-Ireland Club Championship?

15. Who scored the winning point for St. Brigid's in the 2013 All-Ireland Final?

16. Can you name the Carlow club that lost the 1993 All-Ireland Club Final?

17. Which club won an All-Ireland title during the 2000s despite scoring only 0–7 in the final?

18. With which club did Michael Meehan win an All-Ireland Club Championship?

19. Which was the first Kerry club to win the All-Ireland Club Championship?
    a) East Kerry
    b) Dr. Crokes
    c) Laune Rangers

20. Which club did Crossmaglen Rangers beat after a replay in the 2012 All-Ireland Final?
    a) St. Brigid's
    b) Garrycastle
    c) Dr. Crokes

MEDIUM

Answers to Quiz 58: Club Hurling

1. Tommy Moore
2. Roscommon
3. Newtownshandrum
4. Buffer's Alley
5. Ollie Canning
6. Camross
7. De La Salle
8. Crumlin
9. 1995
10. Loughiel Shamrocks
11. Galway
12. Graigue-Ballycallan
13. Mount Leinster Rangers
14. Blackrock
15. Ballyhale Shamrocks
16. Four
17. Birr
18. 1971
19. a) Sixmilebridge
20. c) 7

Quiz 60: Controversies

1. Can you name the Dublin player who was sent off twice during the 1995 All-Ireland Final?

2. Who 'scored' Meath's only goal in the 2010 Leinster Football Final?

3. Which manager described his own players as 'sheep in a heap' after they lost a provincial final?

4. Paul Galvin slapped the notebook out of the hands of which referee during the 2008 Munster Championship?

5. In which year did Cork fail to reappear for extra time in a National League Quarter-Final against Dublin?

6. Can you name the GAA patron who was expelled from the GAA for attending an international soccer match while acting in his official capacity as President of Ireland?

7. By what name has the Tyrone v Dublin National Football League game in 2006 become known?

8. In the 1999 Munster Championship, Kerry was awarded a goal that rebounded off the stanchion against which county?

9. Can you name the Galway player who was banned for a year in 1989 for playing a match in America?

10. Can you name the player who admitted in his autobiography that he went out with the intention of injuring an opposing player during an All-Ireland Final in the 2000s?

11. Laois offered which county a replay during the 1990s after being awarded a point that was later deemed to have been wide?

12. With which club did Seánie Johnston line out in the 2012 Kildare Senior Hurling Championship?

13. Which referee prematurely blew the full-time whistle during the 1998 All-Ireland Hurling Semi-Final?

14. Can you name the Waterford player who was banned from the 1963 League Final because he attended a dance that was run by a soccer club?

15. Can you name the hurler who was sent off during three consecutive championships during the 2000s?

16. In which year did the pre-match brawl known as 'Semplegate' occur between Cork and Clare?

17. Name the Kerry brothers who were both sent off in the 1965 All-Ireland Football Final.

18. In 2003, Seán Óg Ó hAilpín, Damien Fitzhenry, and Paul Codd used hurleys that carried the branding of which company?

19. In which year did three Dublin players get sent off during an All-Ireland Final?
    a) 1977   b) 1979   c) 1983

20. How many players were sent off during the 1999 Leinster Championship clash between Westmeath and Carlow?
    a) 5   b) 6   c) 7

MEDIUM

Answers to Quiz 59: Club Football

1. Cork	11. Laune Rangers
2. Thomond College	12. St. Gall's
3. 1997	13. Three
4. Wexford	14. 1990
5. Corofin	15. Frankie Dolan
6. Ger Brennan	16. Éire Óg
7. Nemo Rangers	17. Salthill-Knocknacarra
8. Kilmacud Crokes	18. Caltra
9. UCD	19. a) East Kerry
10. Walterstown	20. b) Garrycastle

Quiz 61: Young Guns

1. What age was Pat Spillane when he lifted the Sam Maguire Cup as stand-in Kerry captain in 1975?

2. Can you name the Kilkenny player who played a Minor and Senior All-Ireland Final in 1959?

3. In which year did Henry Shefflin win an All-Ireland Under-21 medal?

4. Can you name the Waterford hurler who started his first championship game for his county a few days before he got his Leaving Certificate results in 2010?

5. What age was Donegal player Patrick McBrearty when he scored 1–3 against Cavan in the 2011 Ulster Championship?

6. In which year during the 1990s did the All-Stars Young Footballer of the Year captain his county in an All-Ireland Final?

7. Can you name the Clare 19-year-old who scored 3–3 in the 2013 All-Ireland Final Replay?

8. Who won the All-Stars Young Footballer of the Year Award in both 2011 and 2012?

9. Name the only Tyrone footballer to have won the All-Stars Young Player of the Year and All-Stars Player of the Year?

10. Can you name the Tipperary hurler who won the All-Stars Young Hurler of the Year twice during the 2000s?

11. Niall Tinney won the All-Stars Young Footballer of the Year in 2004 while playing for which county?

12. Can you name the 19-year-old who scored three points for Armagh in the 2002 All-Ireland Football Final?

13. Who was the Dublin player who won the Cadbury's Hero of the Future Award following his side's victory in the 2010 All-Ireland Under-21 Football Championship?

14. Can you name the Kerry player who won an All-Ireland Senior Championship before winning an All-Ireland Minor Championship?

15. Who was the youngest of Kilkenny's seven All-Ireland-winning captains during the 2000s?

16. Who was the first player to win the All-Stars Young Hurler of the Year and Hurler of the Year awards in the same year?

17. Can you name the Dublin player who was awarded the All-Stars Young Hurler of the Year Award in 2011?

18. Can you name the Dublin footballer who won the All-Stars Young Footballer of the Year Award in 2013?

19. Which of these All-Ireland-winning captains was youngest when he received the Sam Maguire Cup?
    a) Michael Murphy
    b) Gary Fahy
    c) Liam Hassett

20. What age was Tipperary's Claire Grogan when she won her first All-Ireland Camogie Championship in 2000?
    a) 14   b) 15   c) 16

MEDIUM

Answers to Quiz 60: Controversies

1. Charlie Redmond
2. Joe Sheridan
3. Michael 'Babs' Keating
4. Paddy Russell
5. 1987
6. Douglas Hyde
7. The Battle of Omagh
8. Tipperary
9. Tony Keady
10. Tadhg Kennelly
11. Carlow
12. Coill Dubh
13. Jimmy Cooney
14. Tom Cheasty
15. Liam Dunne
16. 2007
17. Derry and John O'Shea
18. Paddy Power
19. c) 1983
20. b) 6

Quiz 62: Camogie

1. Can you name the Cork player who scored a hat-trick of goals in the 1993 All-Ireland Final?

2. Who scored Galway's only goal in the 2013 All-Ireland Camogie Final?

3. Can you name the Wexford player who scored 2–7 in the 2012 All-Ireland Final?

4. For which club did Angela Downey score four goals in the 1994 All-Ireland Club Camogie Championship Final?

5. In which year did Dublin last win the All-Ireland Camogie Championship?

6. Who was the first female manager to win an All-Ireland Camogie Championship?

7. Camogie Team of the Century midfielder Mairéad McAtamney played for which county?

8. Can you name the TD who refereed the first All-Ireland Camogie Final?

9. Gretta Quigley captained which county to All-Ireland success on the day after she got married?

10. In which county would you find the Deirdre Camogie Club?

11. Which club has won the All-Ireland Club Camogie Championship the most times?

12. The winners of which camogie championship are awarded the Kay Mills Cup?

13. Which county won its first All-Ireland title in 1974?

14. Can you name the member of the Camogie Team of the Century who has won 64 basketball caps for Ireland?

15. Dublin native Aileen Lawlor was elected President of the Camogie Association in 2011 representing which county?

16. Dublin won the All-Ireland in 1948 with players from which club only?

17. How many All-Ireland medals did Kathleen Mills win during her career with Dublin?

18. Which former hurling All-Star managed Tipperary to a three-in-a-row of All-Ireland camogie titles in 1999, 2000, and 2001?

19. Starting in 1985, how many consecutive All-Ireland titles did Kilkenny win?
    a) 7
    b) 8
    c) 9

20. In which year was the All-Ireland Camogie Final first televised live?
    a) 1988
    b) 1993
    c) 1998

Answers to Quiz 61: Young Guns

1.	19	11.	Fermanagh
2.	Eddie Keher	12.	Rónán Clarke
3.	1999	13.	Rory O'Carroll
4.	Brian O'Halloran	14.	Geraldine O'Shea
5.	17	15.	James 'Cha' Fitzpatrick
6.	1999 (Philip Clifford)	16.	Tony Kelly
7.	Shane O'Donnell	17.	Liam Rushe
8.	Cillian O'Connor	18.	Jack McCaffrey
9.	Seán Cavanagh	19.	c) Liam Hassett
10.	Eoin Kelly	20.	a) 14

Quiz 63: Ladies' Football

1. Can you name the club that won ten All-Ireland Club Championships during the 1980s and 1990s?

2. What is the name of the cup awarded to the winners of the premier third-level ladies' football competition?

3. In which year did Dublin win its first All-Ireland title?

4. Can you name the Cork manager who has guided the county to eight All-Ireland titles?

5. Which county won its first All-Ireland title in 2001?

6. Annette Clarke captained which county to All-Ireland success during the 2000s?

7. What is the name of the official ladies' football magazine?

8. Assumpta Cullen and Leona Tector were both All-Star Award winners from which county?

9. The winners of which competition receive the Mary Quinn Memorial Cup?

10. Which county was the first winner of the All-Ireland Senior Ladies' Football Championship in 1974?

11. Louise Ní Mhuircheartaigh is a sharp-shooting forward for which county?

12. Which county has won the Ladies' National Football League on the most occasions?

13. Patricia O'Brien-Mimna won five All-Star Awards while playing for which two county teams?

14. Can you name the only Dublin club to have won the All-Ireland Club Championship?

15. Up to 2013, how many All-Star Awards has Mayo's Cora Staunton won?

16. In which year did Monaghan win the Ladies' Football All-Ireland for the first time?

17. @Goldieface is the Twitter handle of which ladies' football All-Star?

18. Who was the inaugural Players' Player of the Year Award winner in 2011?

19. In which year was the All-Ireland Final last decided after a replay?
    a) 1998
    b) 2003
    c) 2008

20. Which of these counties has never appeared in a Senior All-Ireland Final?
    a) Leitrim
    b) Donegal
    c) Westmeath

MEDIUM

Answers to Quiz 62: Camogie

1. Lynn Dunlea
2. Ailish O'Reilly
3. Ursula Jacob
4. Lisdowney
5. 1984
6. Stellah Sinnott
7. Antrim
8. Stephen Jordan
9. Wexford
10. Antrim
11. St. Paul's
12. All-Ireland Junior
13. Kilkenny
14. Sandie Fitzgibbon
15. Westmeath
16. CIE Camogie
17. 15
18. Michael Cleary
19. a) 7
20. c) 1998

Quiz 64: Third-Level Competitions

1. Which college has won the Ashbourne Cup on the most occasions?

2. Which college appeared in its only Sigerson Cup Final in 1981?

3. In which year did St. Mary's University Belfast win its first Sigerson Cup?

4. Can you name the 1987 Sigerson-Cup-winning captain who later lifted the Sam Maguire Cup as All-Ireland-winning captain?

5. Who is the only player to captain two different colleges to Sigerson Cup success?

6. Can you name the only university to have completed a six-in-a-row of Sigerson Cup success?

7. Which was the first institute of technology or regional technical college to win the Sigerson Cup?

8. In which two years did UCD win both the Sigerson Cup and the All-Ireland Club Championship?

9. How many consecutive Fitzgibbon Cups did UCC win during the 1980s?

10. Can you name the player who has won a record eight Sigerson Cup medals?

11. Which college won a five-in-a-row of Ashbourne Cups from 2009 to 2013?

12. How was the Sigerson Cup Quarter-Final of 2006 between Sligo IT and UUJ eventually settled?

13. Can you name the former Ireland rugby international who captained UCC to Sigerson Cup success in 1970?

14. Which college won the Ashbourne Cup in 1985 on a scoreline of 8–0 to 0–6?

15. Who wrote the 2013 book *The Cups that Cheered*, which is a history of the Sigerson, Fitzgibbon, and higher education competitions?

16. In which year did Queen's University Belfast win its first Fitzgibbon Cup?

17. With which college did Joe Canning win a Fitzgibbon Cup in 2007?

18. What is the name of the cup awarded to the winners of the second tier of third-level football?

19. Which of these 1980s All-Ireland-winning captains was not on the UCG team that won the 1977 Fitzgibbon Cup?
a) Bobby Ryan   b) Conor Hayes   c) Pat Fleury

20. Which one of these Dublin All-Ireland winners has not captained DCU to Sigerson Cup success?
a) Bryan Cullen   b) Paddy Andrews   c) Paul Flynn

MEDIUM

Answers to Quiz 63: Ladies' Football

1. Ballymacarbry	11. Kerry
2. O'Connor Cup	12. Kerry
3. 2010	13. Cavan and London
4. Éamonn Ryan	14. Ballyboden St. Enda's
5. Laois	15. Nine
6. Galway	16. 1996
7. *Peil*	17. Sinéad Goldrick
8. Wexford	18. Juliet Murphy
9. All-Ireland Intermediate	19. a) 1998
10. Tipperary	20. b) Donegal

Quiz 65: Record Breakers

1. Which club has won its county championship on more occasions than any other club in the country?

2. As of 2013, which former intercounty hurler has the record for the most appearances in championship hurling?

3. Can you name the footballer with the most All-Star Awards?

4. Can you name the only Tipperary hurler with eight All-Ireland Senior Hurling medals?

5. In which year did the All-Ireland Football Final feature two teams from the same province for the first time?

6. Can you name the Waterford player with the most All-Stars?

7. Which county has played in an All-Ireland Hurling Semi-Final on more occasions than any other?

8. Which was the first county to win the All-Ireland Senior Hurling Championship having already lost a game in that year's championship?

9. Which two counties have appeared in but never lost an All-Ireland Football Final?

10. In which year did Christy Ring win his last All-Ireland Senior Hurling Championship?

11. Which Galway hurler won five Hurling All-Star Awards?

12. Who is the all-time top scorer in the All-Ireland Senior Hurling Championship?

13. As of 2013, how many All-Ireland Senior Football Championships has Kerry won?

14. Can you name the player who won seven consecutive All-Ireland Poc Fada Championships?

15. Who is the only player to have won six consecutive All-Ireland medals between football and hurling?

16. Which county had the longest gap between appearances in All-Ireland Senior Football Finals?

17. Which county has won the National Football League on the most occasions?

18. Which footballer is the all-time top scorer in the Ulster Senior Football Championship?

19. Which one of these Kerry players does not have eight All-Ireland medals?
    a) Ger Power
    b) Pat Spillane
    c) Jack O'Shea

20. Which was the first county to win ten All-Ireland Senior Football Championships?
    a) Tipperary
    b) Dublin
    c) Kerry

MEDIUM

Answers to Quiz 64: Third-Level Competitions

1. UCD
2. Trinity College
3. 1989
4. DJ Kane
5. Jim McGuinness
6. UCG
7. Tralee RTC
8. 1974 and 1975
9. Eight
10. Mick Raftery
11. Waterford IT
12. By a penalty shoot-out
13. Moss Keane
14. UCC
15. Dónal McAnallen
16. 1953
17. Limerick IT
18. Trench Cup
19. a) Bobby Ryan
20. c) Paul Flynn

Quiz 66: In Which Year?

1. In which year were Down All-Ireland Football Champions and Offaly All-Ireland Hurling Champions?

2. In which year did Mayo last win the All-Ireland Football Championship?

3. In which year did Dublin last play in an All-Ireland Hurling Final?

4. In which year was the All-Ireland Football Final played in the Polo Grounds in New York?

5. In which year did Derry play in the All-Ireland Final for the first time?

6. In which year did Seán Boylan win his first All-Ireland as Meath manager?

7. In which year did Brian Cody manage Kilkenny in an All-Ireland Final for the first time?

8. In which year were soccer and rugby matches first played in Croke Park?

9. In which year did Paddy Cullen save a penalty from Liam Sammon in an All-Ireland Final?

10. In which year did Christy Ring won his first All-Ireland medal?

11. In which year did Longford win its only Leinster Football Championship?

12. In which year were the All-Star Awards introduced?

13. In which year did Offaly win the All-Ireland Hurling Championship for the first time?

14. In which year did Dublin win the Ladies' Football All-Ireland Championship for the first time?

15. In which year did Jimmy Deenihan captain Kerry to All-Ireland success?

16. In which year did Tony Browne win the All-Star Hurler of the Year Award?

17. In which year did it take four games to separate Dublin and Meath in the Leinster Senior Football Championship?

18. In which year did Louth last appear in a Leinster Football Final?

19. In which year did Mick O'Dwyer stand down as Kerry manager?
    a) 1987   b) 1989   c) 1991

20. In which year did Joe Kernan play in an All-Ireland Final?
    a) 1967   b) 1972   c) 1977

MEDIUM

Answers to Quiz 65: Record Breakers

1. Crossmaglen Rangers
2. Brendan Cummins
3. Pat Spillane
4. John Doyle
5. 2003
6. John Mullane
7. Galway
8. Offaly (1998)
9. Limerick and Donegal
10. 1954
11. Joe Cooney
12. Henry Shefflin
13. 36
14. Ger Cunningham
15. Jack Lynch
16. Kildare (63 years)
17. Kerry
18. Oisín McConville
19. c) Jack O'Shea
20. b) Dublin

Difficult Quizzes

Quiz 67: Pot Luck

1. Can you name the former Tánaiste with an All-Ireland medal?

2. Which club provided three All-Ireland-winning captains during the 2000s?

3. The winners of the Interprovincial Hurling Championship receive which cup?

4. Which Kerry player was Man of the Match in three All-Ireland Football Finals?

5. Can you name the club that hosts the annual Senior All-Ireland Sevens on the eve of the All-Ireland Finals?

6. Can you name the former Dublin player who played in 70 consecutive championship matches during his career?

7. Owenbeg is the Centre of Excellence for which county?

8. Who was the last captain to be presented with the old Liam MacCarthy Cup during the 1990s?

9. In which year did Ger Loughnane step down as manager of the Clare senior hurling team?

10. Who was manager of the Ireland International Rules team in 2013?

11. What is the name of the Leinster hurling competition that is played in January and February?

12. Sam Maguire was a native of which county?

13. Can you name the former Galway hurler with four All-Stars and no All-Ireland medal?

14. In which year did Cavan last win the All-Ireland Senior Football Championship?

15. Which college did Kilkenny full-back JJ Delaney captain to Fitzgibbon Cup success?

16. Who managed the Galway camogie team to All-Ireland success in 2013?

17. Who is the last goalkeeper to lift the Liam MacCarthy Cup as All-Ireland-winning captain?

18. Who was President of the GAA during its centenary year?

19. The Connacht Club Football Championship Cup is named after the son of which former Eurovision winner?
    a) Johnny Logan
    b) Paul Harrington
    c) Charlie McGettigan

20. How many Connacht clubs have won the All-Ireland Club Championship?
    a) 6   b) 8   c) 10

Answers to Quiz 100: Pot Luck

1. Declan Ryan
2. Gary Connaughton
3. 2001
4. Tyrone
5. Thurles Sarsfields
6. Armagh
7. Laois
8. Mullingar Shamrocks
9. Naomh Olaf
10. George Glynn
11. Trevor Giles
12. Mattie McDonagh
13. Nemo Rangers
14. Cormac McAnellan Cup
15. Malainn
16. Sylvie Linnane
17. 1971
18. Teddy McCarthy
19. b) 40
20. b) Kerry

DIFFICULT

Quiz 68: Antrim

1. Who was the Antrim football manager who brought the team to the Ulster Final in 2009?

2. Can you name the former Antrim hurler who won a Dublin Senior Championship with St. Vincent's in 1993?

3. Can you name the Antrim midfielder who won a hurling All-Star Award in 1993?

4. Which Antrim club plays its home games in Páirc Mac Ruairí?

5. The Ulster Club Senior Football Championship Cup is named after which prominent Antrim official?

6. For which Belfast club did international soccer player Gerry Armstrong play in the early 1970s?

7. Can you name the Antrim native who started playing for the Cork footballers in 2013?

8. In which year did Antrim first appear in an All-Ireland Hurling Final?

9. Which county did the Antrim Under-21 hurlers beat in the All-Ireland Semi-Final of 2013?

10. Can you name the Loughiel Shamrocks player who scored 3–7 in the All-Ireland Club Hurling Final in 2012?

11. How many All-Ireland Senior Camogie titles does Antrim have?

12. Who played full-forward on the Antrim side that was defeated in the 1989 All-Ireland Final?

13. Can you name the Antrim man who was President of the GAA from 1938 to 1943?

14. Where in Antrim is the St. Ergnat's club based?

15. In which year did Antrim win its first All-Ireland Under-21 Football Championship?

16. Which Antrim club won the All-Ireland Junior Club Hurling Championship in 2014?

17. In which year did St. Gall's win the All-Ireland Club Football Championship for the first time?

18. Six members of the Donnelly family played in the All-Ireland Club Hurling Final in 1980, representing which club?

19. As of 2014, which Antrim club has won the Senior Club Football Championship the most times?
    a) St. Gall's
    b) O'Donovan Rossa
    c) St. John's

20. In which year did Antrim first compete in the Leinster Senior Hurling Championship?
    a) 2009
    b) 2010
    c) 2011

Answers to Quiz 67: Pot Luck

1. John P Wilson
2. Ballyhale Shamrocks
3. M Donnelly Cup
4. Pat Spillane
5. Kilmacud Crokes
6. John O'Leary
7. Derry
8. Declan Carr
9. 2000
10. Paul Earley
11. Walsh Cup
12. Cork
13. Ollie Canning
14. 1952
15. Waterford IT
16. Tony Ward
17. Noel Skehan
18. Paddy Buggy
19. c) Charlie McGettigan
20. a) 6

DIFFICULT

Quiz 69: Armagh

1. In which year did Armagh first appear in an All-Ireland Senior Football Final?

2. How many All-Star Awards did Stevie McDonnell win during his career?

3. Who was the manager who led the Orchard County to the All-Ireland Final in 1977?

4. Which Armagh club plays its home games at Keeley Park?

5. Can you name the Armagh player who famously missed a penalty in the 1953 All-Ireland Final?

6. In which year did Armagh appear in its first Ladies' Football All-Ireland Final?

7. Who knocked Crossmaglen Rangers out of the 2009 Armagh Championship?

8. How many Ulster Senior Championships did Armagh win during the 2000s?

9. Which Armagh player finished top scorer in the 1993 Ulster Championship?

10. For which Australian Rules club did Dromintee player Kevin Dyas sign in 2007?

11. How many Armagh players won an All-Star Award in 2002?

12. Which county did Armagh defeat after a replay in the 2002 All-Ireland Quarter-Final?

13. Who was 1953 corner-back Gene Morgan's nephew who won an All-Ireland medal in 2002?

14. Who captained Armagh to Nicky Rackard Cup success in 2010?

15. In which year did Armagh win the All-Ireland Minor Championship for the first time?

16. Who captained Armagh to the Ulster Championship title in 1999?

17. For which club did Armagh midfielder Paul McGrane play?

18. Former Armagh goalkeeper Benny Tierney played for which club team?

19. Who succeeded Joe Kernan as Armagh manager in 2007?
    a) Paddy O'Rourke
    b) Paul Grimley
    c) Peter McDonnell

20. In which year did Armagh win the National Football League title for the first time?
    a) 1985
    b) 1995
    c) 2005

Answers to Quiz 68: Antrim

1. Liam Bradley
2. Ciarán Barr
3. Paul McKillen
4. Cardinal O'Donnell's GAC
5. Séamus McFerran
6. St. John's
7. James Loughrey
8. 1943
9. Wexford
10. Liam Watson
11. Six
12. Brian Donnelly
13. Pádraig MacNamee
14. Moneyglass
15. 1969
16. Kickhams Creggan
17. 2010
18. Ballycastle McQuillan GAC
19. c) St. John's
20. a) 2009

DIFFICULT

Quiz 70: Carlow

1. In which year did Carlow win its first Leinster Senior Championship?

2. Which is the only Carlow club to complete a double of Senior Football and Hurling Championship victories?

3. Who captained Carlow to its 2008 Christy Ring Cup success?

4. In which year did Knockbeg College win its first Hogan Cup?

5. True or false: a Carlow man has never held the position of GAA President?

6. Ireland rugby international Seán O'Brien was a selector for which Carlow club that won the 2012 Intermediate Championship?

7. Who defeated Carlow in the 2011 Leinster Football Championship Semi-Final?

8. Who in 2013 became the first Carlow club to win the Leinster Club Hurling Championship?

9. Can you name the Fine Gael TD who served as Carlow County Board Chairman from 2005 to 2010?

10. Which club did Éire Óg defeat after three matches in the 1998 Leinster Club Final?

11. For which Australian Rules club did Brendan Murphy play from 2007 to 2009?

12. In which year did Carlow reach the Leinster Minor Football Championship Final for the first time?

13. Can you name the dual star who was chosen at midfield on the Carlow Hurling Team of the Century and at centre-forward on the Carlow Football Team of the Century?

14. Can you name the Carlow dual star who was awarded the GAA Footballer of the Month Award in May 2004?

15. From whom did Anthony Rainbow take over as Carlow Senior Football manager?

16. Which club plays its home games at Brother Leo Park?

17. Knockbeg College teacher Fr. Paddy Shine brought the school jerseys to which Carlow club, which gave it its colours?

18. Which Carlow club won the Leinster Club Football Championship in 2000?

19. In which year did Mount Leinster Rangers win its first Carlow Senior Hurling Championship?
    a) 2006   b) 2008   c) 2010

20. Which club has won the most Carlow Senior Hurling Championships?
    a) Carlow Town   b) Naomh Eoin   c) St. Mullin's

Answers to Quiz 69: Armagh

1. 1953
2. Three
3. Gerry O'Neill
4. Silverbridge Harps
5. Bill McCorry
6. 2006
7. Pearse Óg
8. Six
9. John Toner
10. Collingwood
11. Six
12. Sligo
13. Oisín McConville
14. Paul McCormack
15. 1949
16. Jarlath Burns
17. Ballyhegan Davitts
18. Mullaghbawn Cúchullains GFC
19. c) Peter McDonnell
20. c) 2005

DIFFICULT

Quiz 71: Cavan

1. Prior to 1997, when did Cavan last win the Ulster Championship?

2. Can you name the Cavan player who scored twelve goals in the Ulster Championship in a career that spanned from 1997 to 2008?

3. In which year did Cavan play Kerry in the All-Ireland Final in New York?

4. Can you name the Cavan player who scored nine points on his Championship debut against Armagh in 2013?

5. Who beat Cavan in the 2011 All-Ireland Under-21 Football Final?

6. Up to 2013, how many Ulster Senior Football Championships have Cavan won?

7. Which club won the Cavan Senior Football Championship for the first time in 2013?

8. What is Aogán Ó Fearghaíl's home club?

9. Can you name the Cavan centre-back who won an All-Star Award in 1978?

10. Whom did Terry Hyland succeed as Cavan manager in 2012?

11. Which Cavan club lost the Ulster Senior Club Finals in 1987 and 1990?

12. Which Cavan player moved from his home club Cúchullains to Dublin's St. Sylvester's in 2013?

13. Who led Cavan to the Ulster Minor Championship in 2011?

14. Can you name the Cornafean man who captained Cavan to All-Ireland success in 1947 and 1948?

15. Can you name the 1947 All-Ireland winner who was Tanáiste from 1990 to 1993?

16. Which Cavan club plays at Max McGrath Park?

17. In which year did St. Patrick's College win the Hogan Cup?

18. Which club brought Mullahoran's 21-year hold on the Cavan Senior Hurling Championship to an end in 2011?

19. Which Ulster Championship winner won an All-Star Award in 1997?
    a) Stephen King
    b) Dermot McCabe
    c) Ronan Carloan

20. In which year did Cavan last contest the National Football League Division One Final?
    a) 1987
    b) 1998
    c) 2002

Answers to Quiz 70: Carlow

1. 1944
2. Naomh Eoin (1986)
3. Edward Coady
4. 2005
5. True
6. Fighting Cocks
7. Wexford
8. Mount Leinster Rangers
9. Pat Deering
10. Kilmacud Crokes
11. Sydney Swans
12. 2007
13. Paddy Quirke
14. Johnny Nevin
15. Luke Dempsey
16. Tullow GAA
17. Tinryland
18. O'Hanrahan's
19. a) 2006
20. c) St. Mullin's

DIFFICULT

Quiz 72: Clare

1. In which year did Clare win the All-Ireland Senior Hurling Championship for the first time?

2. Can you name the Clare hurler who won All-Star Hurler of the Year and Young Hurler of the Year in 2013?

3. Which Clare club is known as the Magpies?

4. Which former Clare hurler released an autobiography entitled *Screaming at the Sky*?

5. Which former Kerry player managed the Clare footballers in 2007?

6. Who scored Clare's fourth goal in the 2013 All-Ireland Hurling Final replay?

7. Which is the most westerly GAA club in county Clare?

8. Who captained Clare in the 2002 All-Ireland Hurling Final?

9. Can you name the Clare side who won the 1999 All-Ireland Club Hurling Championship?

10. How many Munster Senior Hurling Championships did Ger Loughnane win as Clare manager?

11. Who managed Clare to two National League titles in the 1970s?

12. In which year did Clare win the Under-21 All-Ireland Hurling Championship for the first time?

13. Name the man who began his reign as Clare Senior Football Manager in 2014.

14. Which club won the Clare Senior Hurling Championship for the first time in 2009?

15. Which county did Clare beat in the 1997 All-Ireland Semi-Final?

16. Who scored Clare's only goal in the 1995 All-Ireland Hurling Final?

17. Who in 2009 became the first Clare club to contest the All-Ireland Club Football Final?

18. Who was the Clare All-Ireland-winning Minor Hurling captain in 1997?

19. Which county did Clare beat in the 1995 Munster Hurling Final?
    a) Limerick
    b) Tipperary
    c) Cork

20. Which Clare player won the All-Star Hurler of the Year Award in 1995?
    a) Anthony Daly
    b) Seán McMahon
    c) Brian Lohan

Answers to Quiz 71: Cavan

1.	1969	11.	Kingscourt Stars
2.	Jason Reilly	12.	Eugene Keating
3.	1947	13.	Gary Donahoe
4.	Martin Dunne	14.	John Joe O'Reilly
5.	Galway	15.	John Wilson
6.	37	16.	Redhills
7.	Ballinagh	17.	1972
8.	Éire Óg Drumgoon	18.	Ballymachugh
9.	Ollie Brady	19.	b) Dermot McCabe
10.	Val Andrews	20.	c) 2002

DIFFICULT

Quiz 73: Cork

1. How many consecutive All-Ireland Championships did the Cork Ladies' Football team win during the 2000s?

2. For which club did Jack Lynch play hurling?

3. Who captained Cork to All-Ireland success in 2010?

4. In which year did Jimmy Barry-Murphy win his only All-Ireland Football Championship?

5. Which Cork hurler was selected as All-Star Hurler of the Year in 1999?

6. Who took charge of the Cork Senior Football team in October 2013?

7. Can you name the Cork camogie player who scored two goals in two minutes in the 1998 All-Ireland Final?

8. Who scored Cork's only goal in the 2005 All-Ireland Senior Hurling Final?

9. In which Cork town is there a statue of Sam Maguire?

10. Up to 2014, how many All-Ireland Club Football Championships has Nemo Rangers won?

11. Which county did Cork beat in the 1989 All-Ireland Football Final?

12. How many All-Ireland medals did Christy Ring win?

13. Can you name the Cork hurler who scored a late goal against Tipperary in the 1984 Munster Final?

14. Which Cork club completed a double of Munster Senior Football and Hurling Club Championships in 1980?

15. Diarmuid O'Sullivan and Donal Óg Cusack play hurling with which club?

16. In which year did Gerald McCarthy captain Cork to All-Ireland success?

17. In which West Cork town is the O'Donovan Rossa Club based?

18. In which year did Seán Óg Ó hAilpín captain Cork to All-Ireland success?

19. How many Cork hurlers were chosen on the GAA Team of the Millennium?
    a) Three
    b) Four
    c) Five

20. Who was Cork's first football All-Star in 1971?
    a) Frank Cogan
    b) Ray Cummins
    c) Kevin Jer O'Sullivan

Answers to Quiz 72: Clare

1. 1914
2. Tony Kelly
3. Clarecastle
4. Tony Griffin
5. Páidí Ó Sé
6. Conor McGrath
7. Naomh Eoin
8. Brian Lohan
9. St. Joseph's Doora-Barefield
10. Three
11. Justin McCarthy
12. 2009
13. Colm Collins
14. Cratloe
15. Kilkenny
16. Éamonn Taaffe
17. Kilmurry Ibrickane
18. John Reddan
19. a) Limerick
20. c) Brian Lohan

DIFFICULT

Quiz 74: Derry

1. In which year did Derry first appear in an All-Ireland Football Final?

2. Which club plays at Dean McGlinchey Park?

3. Who was the Derry goalkeeper in the 1993 All-Ireland Football Final?

4. How many All-Star Awards did Tony Scullion win during his career?

5. The Derry hurlers won their first Ulster Senior Championship after a gap of 92 years in which year?

6. Which Derry player was chosen as full-forward on the 2004 All-Star team?

7. Which Derry club has won the Senior Hurling Championship the most times?

8. How many separate stints did Mickey Moran have as Derry manager?

9. With which club side does Seán Marty Lockhart play?

10. Who was Derry football manager from 1991 to 1994?

11. Can you name the former Derry player who managed the Ireland International Rules Football team from 2010 to 2011?

12. Can you name the Dungiven man who won a Nicky Rackard Cup with the Derry hurlers in 2006 and a National League with the footballers in 2008?

13. How many National Football League titles did Derry win during the 1990s?

14. Which Derry club competed in the first series of *Celebrity Bainisteoir* in 2008?

15. Who sponsored Derry when it won the All-Ireland title in 1993?

16. Up to 2013, how many Hogan Cup titles has St. Patrick's College, Maghera, won?

17. Who was captain of the All-Ireland-winning Derry minor team in 2002?

18. Which Derry player was chosen as Texaco Footballer of the Year in 1958?

19. Which county did Derry defeat in the 1997 All-Ireland Under-21 Football Final?
    a) Laois
    b) Kerry
    c) Meath

20. Who were the first All-Ireland Club Football Champions from Derry?
    a) Ballinderry Shamrocks
    b) Lavey
    c) Bellaghy

Answers to Quiz 73: Cork

1. Five
2. Glen Rovers
3. Graham Canty
4. 1973
5. Brian Corcoran
6. Brian Cuthbert
7. Irene O'Keeffe
8. Ben O'Connor
9. Dunmanway
10. Seven
11. Mayo
12. Eight
13. Seánie O'Leary
14. St. Finbarr's
15. Cloyne
16. 1966
17. Skibbereen
18. 2005
19. a) Three
20. b) Ray Cummins

DIFFICULT

Quiz 75: Donegal

1. Who was Donegal's first All-Star in 1972?

2. Can you name the Donegal player who scored the winning point against Kildare in the 2011 All-Ireland Quarter-Final?

3. Which is the most southerly GAA Club in County Donegal?

4. Which county did Donegal defeat in the 1992 All-Ireland Semi-Final?

5. In which year did Donegal win the All-Ireland Under-21 Football Championship for the first time?

6. Who sang the 2012 song 'Jimmy's Winning Matches'?

7. Which Donegal club has won the Donegal Senior Hurling Championship the most times?

8. Which is the only Donegal club to have won the Ulster Senior Club Championship?

9. Can you name the Donegal man who captained Sligo IT to Sigerson Cup success in 2005?

10. Can you name the Fermanagh native who was a selector on the Donegal team during its 2012 All-Ireland success?

11. What is the home club of former Donegal player Joyce McMullan

12. Which county did Donegal defeat in the replayed 2003 All-Ireland Quarter-Final?

13. Can you name the Four Masters clubman who won an All-Star Award in 1974?

14. Can you name the Kilcar brothers who played for Donegal in the 1992 All-Ireland Final?

15. Colm McFadden plays for which Donegal club?

16. Can you name the Donegal player who missed a penalty in the closing minutes of the 2010 All-Ireland Under-21 Championship Final?

17. Which club plays its home games at Davy Brennan Memorial Park?

18. Which Donegal club won its first Senior Championship in 2011?

19. In which year did Donegal win the Nicky Rackard Cup for the first time?
    a) 2009
    b) 2011
    c) 2013

20. By how many points did Donegal beat Mayo in the 2012 All-Ireland Final?
    a) 2   b) 4   c) 6

Answers to Quiz 74: Derry

1.	1958	11.	Anthony Tohill
2.	Ballinascreen	12.	Liam Hinphey
3.	Damien McClusker	13.	Three
4.	Four	14.	St. Mary's Faughanvale
5.	2000	15.	Sperrin Metal
6.	Enda Muldoon	16.	Five
7.	Kevin Lynch's Dungiven	17.	Gerard O'Kane
8.	Three	18.	Jim McKeever
9.	St. Mary's Banagher	19.	c) Meath
10.	Eamonn Coleman	20.	c) Bellaghy

DIFFICULT

Quiz 76: Down

1. In which year did Down lose an All-Ireland Football Final for the first time?

2. For which club did the great Seán O'Neill play?

3. For which club does Brendan Coulter play?

4. Who captained Down to the 1961 All-Ireland title?

5. By what name is Páirc Esler in Newry also known?

6. Can you name the Down forward who scored a late goal to win the 2013 Christy Ring Cup Final against Kerry?

7. Ulster and Ireland rugby player Craig Gilroy played football with which Down club in his youth?

8. In which year did South Down first enter the National Hurling League?

9. Which Down player was selected to the GAA Team of the Millennium?

10. In which year did Down win the Ulster Senior Football Championship for the first time?

11. What is the name of the cup awarded to the winners of the Down Senior Football Championship?

12. Can you name the Down footballer who won two All-Star Awards during the 1970s?

13. Who scored Down's only goal in the 2005 All-Ireland Minor Final?

14. Which county did Down beat in the 1968 All-Ireland Final?

15. Can you name the Down hurler who received a Christy Ring Cup Champion Award for three consecutive years from 2010?

16. Can you name the former Down footballer who won the 60-metre Masters Indoor Championship of Ireland title in 2014?

17. Who managed Down to the 1983 National League title?

18. Which father and son both captained St. Colman's College to McRory Cup success?

19. Which was the first Down club to win the All-Ireland Senior Club Championship?
    a) Burren
    b) Bryansford
    c) Castlewellan

20. Who succeeded Pete McGrath as Down manager in 2002?
    a) Ross Carr
    b) Greg Blaney
    c) Paddy O'Rourke

Answers to Quiz 75: Donegal

1. Brian McEniff
2. Kevin Cassidy
3. Réalt na Mara, Bundoran
4. Mayo
5. 1982
6. Rory and the Island
7. Burt
8. St Joseph's
9. Christy Toye
10. Rory Gallagher
11. Four Masters
12. Galway
13. Donal Monoghan
14. Martin and James McHugh
15. Naomh Mícheál
16. Michael Murphy
17. Naomh Cónaill
18. Glenswilly
19. c) 2013
20. b) 4

DIFFICULT

Quiz 77: Dublin

1. Can you name the 1961 Leinster Championship winner who presented the Bob O'Keeffe Cup to John McCaffrey after the 2013 Leinster Hurling Final?

2. Multiple All-Ireland handball champion Eoin Kennedy plays for which Dublin club?

3. Which Dublin club plays its home games at Ballast Pit?

4. Who scored Dublin's only goal in the 1983 All-Ireland Football Final?

5. In which year did Alan Brogan captain the Dublin Under-21 Football team to All-Ireland success?

6. Who is the last player from a southside club to captain Dublin to All-Ireland success?

7. The song *Fourteen Men*, about the Leinster Final of 1979, was written by which Dublin band?

8. How many All-Star Awards did Dublin goalkeeper John O'Leary win during his career?

9. For which club did Dublin midfielder Ciarán Whelan play?

10. From whom did Anthony Daly take over as Dublin Senior Hurling Manager in 2008?

11. Which club has won the Dublin Senior Hurling Championship a record 31 times?

12. As of 2013, who is the only Dublin hurler to have won two All-Star Awards?

13. Who captained the Dublin Ladies' Football team to All-Ireland success in 2010?

14. Which former Dublin All-Ireland winner was nicknamed the Blue Panther?

15. Can you name the Dublin camogie player who won a record 15 All-Ireland medals?

16. How many All-Ireland Senior Football medals did Kevin Heffernan win as a player?

17. Prior to 2011, in which year did Dublin last win the National Hurling League?

18. What colours does the Fingal Hurling team wear?

19. How many All-Ireland Football Finals did Dublin appear in during the 1990s?
    a) Three   b) Four   c) Five

20. Can you name the Dublin player who won the Man of the Match Award after the 2011 All-Ireland Final?
    a) Paul Flynn   b) Kevin Nolan   c) Barry Cahill

Answers to Quiz 76: Down

1. 2010	11. Frank O'Hare Cup
2. John Mitchel GFC	12. Colm McAlarney
3. Mayobridge	13. Paul McCumiskey
4. Paddy Doherty	14. Kerry
5. The Marshes	15. Paul Braniff
6. Gareth 'Magic' Johnson	16. Mickey Linden
7. St. Paul's	17. James McCartan Snr.
8. 2008	18. Seán and Greg Blaney
9. Seán O'Neill	19. a) Burren
10. 1959	20. c) Paddy O'Rourke

DIFFICULT

Quiz 78: Fermanagh

1. Can you name the Fermanagh man who captained Queen's University to Sigerson success in 1993?

2. Can you name the Fermanagh native who won an All-Ireland Senior Club Championship title in 2010 with St. Gall's?

3. Who was Fermanagh's first All-Star in 1982?

4. For which club does Fermanagh player Martin McGrath play?

5. In what colours do Enniskillen Gaels play?

6. Who was the first Fermanagh man to become President of the GAA?

7. In which year did Fermanagh win the Ulster Under-21 Championship for the first time?

8. Which club won its first Fermanagh Senior Football Championship in 2008?

9. Up to 2014, how many times has Fermanagh won the Dr. McKenna Cup?

10. Can you name the Fermanagh player who scored eleven goals in the Ulster Championship between 1960 and 1973?

11. Who was Fermanagh manager during the run to the Semi-Final of the 2004 Championship?

12. Which Fermanagh club plays at Canon Maguire Park?

13. Who is Fermanagh's only two-time All-Star?

14. With 31 titles, which club has won the Fermanagh Senior Hurling Championship most times?

15. In which year did Fermanagh win the All-Ireland Junior Football Championship?

16. Who served as Fermanagh manager for the 2012 and 2013 seasons?

17. Who became the first Fermanagh player to score a goal in the 2004 All-Ireland Semi-Final?

18. in 1982, which was the first Fermanagh club to play in the Ulster Senior Club Championship Final?

19. Who beat Fermanagh in the 2012 Lory Meagher Cup Final?
    a) Longford
    b) Tyrone
    c) Louth

20. In which year did Fermanagh lose a replay against Armagh in the Ulster Final?
    a) 2004
    b) 2006
    c) 2008

Answers to Quiz 77: Dublin

1. Jimmy Gray
2. St. Brigid's
3. Skerries Harps
4. Barney Rock
5. 2003
6. Seán Doherty
7. The Wolfe Tones
8. Five
9. Raheny
10. Tommy Naughton
11. Faughs
12. Liam Rushe
13. Denise Masterson
14. Anton O'Toole
15. Kathleen Mills
16. One
17. 1939
18. Purple and white
19. a) Three
20. b) Kevin Nolan

DIFFICULT

Quiz 79: Galway

1. Who managed the Galway hurlers to the 2005 All-Ireland Final?

2. Can you name the only Galway player with four All-Ireland Senior Football medals?

3. The book *True Grit* details the career of which former Galway hurler?

4. Who won the 1996 Galway Senior Football Championship for the first time?

5. Can you name the Galway player who was sent off in the 1983 All-Ireland Football Final?

6. How many Connolly brothers were on the Castlegar team that won the 1980 All-Ireland Club Championship?

7. Up to 2013, how many All-Ireland Minor Hurling Championships has Mattie Murphy won as manager?

8. Can you name the Galway hurler who won the Man of the Match Award in the 1993 All-Ireland Final?

9. What is the official name of Tuam Stadium?

10. In which year did Galway win the All-Ireland Camogie Championship for the first time?

11. Can you name the Galway player who won All-Star Footballer of the Year and All-Star Young Footballer of the Year in 1998?

12. Whom did Alan Mulholland succeed as Galway Senior Football Manager?

13. The song *Maroon and White* was performed by which Galway band?

14. Which was the first Galway club to win the All-Ireland Club Football Championship?

Answers – page 165

15. Which Galway All-Ireland winner in 1956 played with Louth during the early 1950s?

16. Can you name the former Galway footballer who directed the documentary *A Year Til Sunday*?

17. Can you name the Galway man who captained UCG to two Fitzgibbon Cup victories?

18. Can you name the Galway footballer who scored two goals in the 2004 All-Ireland Ladies' Football Final?

19. What is Cyril Farrell's home club?
    a) Gort
    b) Mullagh
    c) Tommy Larkins

20. In which year did Galway first win the All-Ireland Senior Football Championship?
    a) 1916   b) 1925   c) 1934

Answers to Quiz 78: Fermanagh

1. Paul Brewster	11. Charlie Mulgrew
2. Rory Gallagher	12. Derrygonnelly Harps
3. Peter McGinnity	13. Barry Owens
4. St. Joseph's	14. Lisbellaw St. Patrick's
5. Blue and gold	15. 1959
6. Peter Quinn	16. Peter Canavan
7. 1970	17. James Sherry
8. St. Patrick's, Donagh	18. Roslea Shamrocks
9. Four	19. b) Tyrone
10. PT Treacy	20. c) 2008

DIFFICULT

Quiz 80: Kerry

1. Can you name the Kerry man who won four All-Ireland medals before he reached his 21st birthday?

2. How many All-Ireland titles did Jack O'Connor win as Kerry manager?

3. The Munster Club Senior Football Championship cup is named after which former Kerry player and administrator?

4. Who was the first Kerry man to become President of the GAA?

5. The Spillane brothers Pat, Mick, and Tom, played with which club?

6. In which year did Mick O'Connell captain Kerry to All-Ireland success?

7. Players from Currow, Cordal, and Scartaglin can play with which divisional side?

8. Whom did Mick O'Dwyer succeed as Kerry manager in 1974?

9. As of 2014, which Kerry club has won the Senior Hurling Championship the most times?

10. How many All-Ireland Senior Football Championships did Kerry win during the 2000s?

11. Which Dingle player was selected at right-half back on the GAA Football Team of the Millennium?

12. In which year did Maurice Fitzgerald make his championship debut for Kerry?

13. Who captained Kerry to All-Ireland success in the centenary year of the GAA?

14. How many goals did Kerry score in the 1978 All-Ireland Final?

15. Between playing and managing, how many All-Ireland successes has Mick O'Dwyer been involved with?

16. Which Kerry club won the All-Ireland Intermediate Club Championship in 2009?

17. Who is the only Kerry player to lift the Sam Maguire Cup twice as captain since the 1940s?

18. Can you name the Kerry father and son who have both won Football All-Star Awards?

19. In which year did Colm Cooper play in a Senior All-Ireland for the first time?
    a) 2000
    b) 2002
    c) 2004

20. Starting in 1982, how many consecutive Ladies' Football All-Ireland Championships did Kerry win?
    a) 6
    b) 7
    c) 8

Answers to Quiz 79: Galway

1. Conor Hayes
2. Mattie McDonagh
3. Sylvie Linnane
4. An Cheathrú Rua
5. Tomás Tierney
6. Five
7. Six
8. Pádraig Kelly
9. St. Jarlath's Park
10. 1996
11. Michael Donnellan
12. Tomás Ó Flatharta
13. The Saw Doctors
14. Corofin
15. Frank Stockwell
16. Pat Comer
17. Miko Doyle
18. Niamh Duggan
19. c) Tommy Larkins
20. b) 1925

DIFFICULT

Quiz 81: Kildare

1. Which was the first Kildare club to win the Leinster Senior Club Championship?

2. Can you name the dual player who was selected to both the Kildare football and hurling teams of the Millennium?

3. For how many Championship campaigns was Kieren McGeeney in charge of Kildare?

4. In which year did Kildare win the All-Ireland Under-21 Football Championship?

5. Which All-Ireland-winning captain took charge of the Kildare hurlers in 2007?

6. To which county did Kildare lose by four points in the 1976 Leinster Senior Hurling Semi-Final?

7. With which club did Larry Tompkins win a Kildare Junior B Championship in 1981?

8. For which hurling club did Seánie Johnston play in the Kildare Senior Hurling Championship?

9. How old was Dermot Earley when he scored a goal in the 1998 All-Ireland Football Final?

10. Which Kildare club won its first Senior Football Championship in 2008?

11. The son of which former Kildare All-Star plays with Meath?

12. Can you name the Kildare player who scored the only goal in the 1998 Leinster Senior Football Final?

13. In how many Leinster Finals did Kildare appear while Kieran McGeeney was manager?

14. The overpass bridge at Leixlip on the Dublin–Galway motorway is named after which former Kildare footballer?

15. Prior to 1998, when did Kildare last win the Leinster Senior Football Championship?

16. Which Kildare club plays its home games at Creighton Park?

17. Can you name the Kildare player who received an All-Star Award in 1991?

18. Can you name the Kildare player who rattled the crossbar with a last-minute free against Down in the 2010 All-Ireland Semi-Final?

19. With which Kildare club did Karl O'Dwyer win a Senior Championship?
    a) Round Towers
    b) Rathangan
    c) Moorefield

20. How many Senior Football All-Ireland Championships has Kildare won?
    a) 3
    b) 4
    c) 5

Answers to Quiz 80: Kerry

1. Miko Doyle
2. Three
3. Michael O'Connor
4. Seán Kelly
5. Templenoe
6. 1959
7. St. Kieran's
8. Johnny Culloty
9. Ballyduff
10. Five
11. Seán Murphy
12. 1988
13. Ambrose O'Donovan
14. Five
15. Twelve
16. St. Michael's/Foilmore
17. Declan O'Sullivan
18. Tim and Tadhg Kennelly
19. b) 2002
20. c) 8

DIFFICULT

Quiz 82: Kilkenny

1. Name DJ Carey's great-uncle, who was chosen for the Hurling Team of the Millennium.

2. In which year did Billy Fitzpatrick captain Kilkenny to All-Ireland success?

3. How many All-Ireland Championship medals did Brian Cody win as a player?

4. Which Kilkenny club plays its home matches in Tom Ryall Park?

5. Can you name the Kilkenny player who scored a hat-trick of goals in the 1959 All-Ireland Hurling Final?

6. In which year did Kilkenny complete a quadruple, by winning the All-Ireland at Senior, Under-21, Minor, and Intermediate?

7. How many All-Ireland Senior Hurling Championships did Kilkenny win during the 1950s?

8. Up to 2013, how many times has Henry Shefflin won the All-Stars Hurler of the Year Award?

9. Can you name the substitute who replaced his brother in an All-Ireland Final during the 2000s?

10. Who managed the Kilkenny Senior Hurling team from 1995 to 1997?

11. The newest stand in Nowlan Park, which opened in 2010, is named after which former Kilkenny player and administrator?

12. How many Kilkenny players were chosen on the Hurling Team of the Millennium?

13. All-Ireland-winning defenders Pa Dillon and Michael Kavanagh played for which Kilkenny club?

Answers – page 171

14. Which Kilkenny player won the Man of the Match Award in the 2006 All-Ireland Final?

15. How many All-Ireland Camogie titles did Angela Downey win?

16. Which Kilkenny player scored 2–3 in the 1982 All-Ireland Final?

17. How many Fennelly brothers lined out for Ballyhale Shamrocks in the 1989 All-Ireland Club Championship Final?

18. In which year did Kilkenny CBS win its first Dr. Croke Cup?

19. Up to 2013, who is Kilkenny's championship top scorer?
a) Eddie Keher
b) DJ Carey
c) Henry Shefflin

20. In which year did Henry Shefflin make his championship debut?
a) 1998   b) 1999   c) 2000

Answers to Quiz 81: Kildare

1. Raheens
2. Tommy Carew
3. Six
4. 1965
5. Andy Comerford
6. Wexford
7. Eadestown
8. Coill Dubh
9. 20
10. Celbridge
11. Davy Dalton
12. Brian Murphy
13. One
14. Matt Goff
15. 1956
16. Confey
17. Martin Lynch
18. Robert Kelly
19. a) Round Towers
20. b) 4

DIFFICULT

169

Quiz 83: Laois

1. Whom did Mick O'Dwyer succeed as Laois Senior Football manager?

2. Which is the only Laois club to have won the Leinster Senior Club Hurling Championship?

3. Who captained Laois to All-Ireland Minor Football success in 2003?

4. Which former Laois player uses the Twitter name 'Woolberto'?

5. Which former Laois player managed Knockbeg College to Hogan Cup success in 2005?

6. Jim Sayers, who won the Leinster Championship with Laois in 1946, had a grandson on the 2003 team. Who was he?

7. In which year did Laois win the All-Ireland Minor Football Championship for the first time?

8. Which Laois player walked in the parade before the 2004 Leinster Final with his son?

9. Up to 2013, how many times has Portlaoise won the Leinster Senior Club Football Championship?

10. With which Laois club did Meath All-Ireland winner Bernard Flynn play?

11. Who is the only Laois hurler to have won an All-Star?

12. Can you name the Laois player who suffered a horrific ankle injury in the All-Ireland Qualifier against Tyrone in 2004?

13. After which famous Laois family is the Leinster Senior Football Championship cup named?

14. Which former Laois hurler is known as 'Cheddar'?

15. Who is the only Laois man to have captained Leinster to Railway Cup success?

16. Which former Laois player was known as 'The Boy Wonder'?

17. Who managed the Laois Ladies' Football team to All-Ireland success in 2001?

18. James Young plays club hurling with which club?

19. In which year did Laois last appear in a Leinster Senior Hurling Final?
    a) 1975
    b) 1985
    c) 1995

20. Which county did Laois beat in the 2003 Leinster Senior Football Semi-Final?
    a) Meath
    b) Dublin
    c) Wexford

Answers to Quiz 82: Kilkenny

1.	Paddy Phelan	11.	Ted Carroll
2.	1975	12.	Four
3.	Three	13.	St. Lachtain's
4.	Graigue-Ballycallan	14.	Aidan Fogarty
5.	Tommy O'Connell	15.	Twelve
6.	2008	16.	Christy Heffernan
7.	One	17.	Seven
8.	Three	18.	1981
9.	Richie Mullally	19.	c) Henry Shefflin
10.	Nickey Brennan	20.	b) 1999

DIFFICULT

Quiz 84: Leitrim

1. In which year did the Leitrim Ladies' Football team compete in the All-Ireland Senior Final?

2. Starting in 1999, how many consecutive Leitrim Senior Hurling Championships did St. Mary's Kiltoghert win?

3. In which year did Leitrim win the All-Ireland B Championship?

4. Can you name the Leitrim player whose senior intercounty career spanned 24 years from 1949 to 1973?

5. Who scored Leitrim's only goal in its 2011 Connacht Championship victory against Sligo?

6. Who was appointed Leitrim Senior Football Manager in September 2013?

7. Which Leitrim club won its first Senior Football Championship in 2005?

8. Can you name the Leitrim referee who took charge of the 1991 All-Ireland Football Final?

9. How many Leitrim players were on the Connacht panel that won the 2014 Interprovincial Final?

10. Leitrim recorded its first win of the All-Ireland Qualifier series against which county in 2012?

11. Which Leitrim club won a three-in-a-row of Senior Football Championships from 1992 to 1994?

12. To which county did Leitrim lose in the 1998 All-Ireland Minor Football Semi-Final?

13. Which former All-Star managed the Leitrim Senior Football team during the 1990s?

14. Which Leitrim club plays its home games in Philly McGuinness Memorial Park?

Answers – page 175

15. Which Leitrim club did Katherine Lynch manage in the second season of *Celebrity Bainisteoir*?

16. In which year did Leitrim last appear in a Connacht Senior Football Final?

17. Who was the first Leitrim player to be selected to the Ireland International Rules team?

18. Can you name the man who captained Leitrim to Connacht Championship success in 1927?

19. In what colours do Melvin Gaels play?
    a) Blue and white
    b) Green and gold
    c) Red and black

20. In which year did Páirc Seán Mac Diarmada open?
    a) 1954
    b) 1964
    c) 1974

Answers to Quiz 83: Laois

1. Colm Browne
2. Camross
3. Craig Rogers
4. Colm Parkinson
5. Chris Conway
6. Pauric Clancy
7. 1996
8. Colm Byrne
9. Seven
10. St. Joseph's
11. Pat Critchley
12. Brian McDonald
13. The Delaneys
14. Seamus Plunkett
15. Bill Delaney
16. Tommy Murphy
17. Mary Ramsbottom
18. Clonaslee-St.Manmans
19. b) 1985
20. b) Dublin

DIFFICULT

Quiz 85: Limerick

1. Who managed Limerick to Munster Senior Hurling Championship success in 2013?

2. How many All-Ireland Senior Hurling Championships did Mick Mackey win?

3. For which Limerick club did Ireland rugby player Seán Cronin play?

4. Which Limerick player scored the winning point with the last puck of the game against Tipperary in the 1973 Munster Hurling Final?

5. Which Limerick club represented the county and won the inaugural All-Ireland Football Championship in 1887?

6. Can you name the Kilkenny native who played for Limerick in the 1974 All-Ireland Final?

7. Limerick brothers Ollie and Niall Moran play with which club side?

8. Which former Limerick player and manager is commemorated by a statue in Annacotty?

9. Which Limerick club won its first Limerick Senior Hurling Championship in 2001?

10. Which Limerick club is nicknamed 'The Bouncers'?

11. In which year did Limerick take Kerry to a replay in the Munster Senior Football Final?

12. Who scored Limerick's only goal in the 1973 All-Ireland Hurling Final?

13. Which Limerick club won the Munster Senior Club Football Championship in 2008?

14. Can you name the Limerick All-Ireland winner who was a Fianna Fáil TD from 1957 to 1969?

15. Which Limerick player scored a hat-trick of goals against Cork in the 1976 Munster Hurling Final?

16. Can you name the Limerick player who scored the winning point, from a free, against Wexford in the 2011 All-Ireland Football Qualifier Round 4?

17. Can you name the Limerick goalkeeper who has won three All-Ireland Under-21 Championships?

18. Can you name the Limerick player who won three All-Star Awards during the 1980s?

19. Who captained Limerick in the 2007 All-Ireland Hurling Final?
a) Stephen Lucey
b) Brian Geary
c) Damien Reale

20. Who managed Limerick in the 1994 All-Ireland Hurling Final?
a) Tom Ryan
b) Éamonn Cregan
c) Phil Bennis

Answers to Quiz 84: Leitrim

1. 1984
2. Twelve
3. 1990
4. Packie McGarty
5. Conor Beirne
6. Seán Hagan
7. Kiltubrid
8. Seamus Prior
9. Three
10. Wicklow
11. Aughawillian
12. Tyrone
13. Peter McGinnity
14. Mohill
15. St. Patrick's Dromahair
16. 2000
17. Séamus Quinn
18. Tom Gannon
19. a) Blue and white
20. b) 1964

DIFFICULT

Quiz 86: Longford

1. Can you name the Longford man who has the Kick Fada world record with a point from 75 metres?

2. Up to 2014, how many Hogan Cups has St. Mel's won?

3. Can you name the Longford man who, in the 1962 Railway Cup Final, became the first footballer to score a point live on television?

4. Who managed the Longford Senior Footballers from 2009 to 2013?

5. Can you name the Longford player who received All-Star nominations in 1988, 1989, and 1990?

6. Which Longford GAA official became Chairman of the Leinster Council in 2011?

7. Can you name the Longford player who was selected to the Ireland International Rules team in 1984?

8. Who scored eight out of his side's nine points for Longford in the 1966 National League Final?

9. Can you name the Longford man who captained UCD to Sigerson Cup success in 1962?

10. Which Longford club plays its home games at Michael Fay Park?

11. Can you name the Longford player who won an All-Ireland Senior Club Championship in 2009?

12. For which Longford club did former Director General of the GAA Liam Mulvihill play?

13. Can you name the All-Ireland-winning captain who coached Longford to a National League and Leinster Championship during the 1960s?

14. In which year did Longford win the Nicky Rackard Cup for the first time?

15. Which Longford club won a three-in-a-row of Senior Club Football Championships during the 1990s?

16. Can you name the Longford father and son who won Interprovincial Championships with Leinster in the 1960s and the 2000s?

17. Who captained Longford to the Leinster Minor Football Championship in 2010?

18. Can you name the All-Ireland-winning manager who managed Longford during the mid-1990s?

19. For which club did former Longford footballer Niall Sheridan play?
a) Clonguish   b) St. Mary's   c) Abbeylara

20. Up to 2014, how many Leinster Minor Football Championships has Longford won?
a) 2   b) 4   c) 6

Answers to Quiz 85: Limerick

1. John Allen
2. Three
3. Monaleen
4. Richie Bennis
5. Limerick Commercials
6. Matt Ruth
7. Ahane
8. Jackie Power
9. Adare
10. Garryspillane
11. 2004
12. Mossie Dowling
13. Drumcollogher-Broadford
14. Paddy Clohessy
15. Éamonn Cregan
16. Ian Ryan
17. Timmy Houlihan
18. Leonard Enright
19. c) Damien Reale
20. a) Tom Ryan

DIFFICULT

Quiz 87: Louth

1. Who was the Louth man who won an Ulster Senior Championship with Monaghan in 1988?

2. For which Australian Rules team did Ciarán Byrne sign in August 2013?

3. Can you name the Louth full-back who won five Railway Cups with Leinster?

4. Can you name the Louth player who scored his side's only goal in the 2010 Leinster Senior Football Final?

5. Which county did Louth defeat in the 2011 Division Three National League Final?

6. Up to 2013, in how many Nicky Rackard Cup Finals has Louth appeared?

7. In which year did Louth win the All-Ireland Senior Football Championship for the first time?

8. Who was Louth's first ever football All-Star?

9. With which Louth club did Ireland soccer international Steve Staunton win a Louth Senior Football Championship during the 1980s?

10. Prior to 2010, when did Louth last appear in a Leinster Senior Football Final?

11. The Leinster Under-21 Football Championship Cup is named after which Louth GAA official?

12. Can you name the Louth man who captained UCD to Sigerson Cup success in 1968?

13. Which Louth club won the 2013 Leinster Intermediate Club Championship?

14. Who captained Louth to the 1957 Leinster Championship?

15. Which Louth club won its only two Senior Football Championships in 1996 and 2006?

16. Can you name the Louth All-Ireland winner who later played for Cavan, winning an Ulster Championship in 1962?

17. Which Louth GAA Club hails from the village of Collon?

18. Can you name the Louth player who was chosen on the GAA Football Team of the Century in 1984?

19. Which Louth club won nine Senior Hurling Championships between 2000 and 2011?
    a) Pearse Óg
    b) Knockbridge
    c) Naomh Moninne

20. In which year did Louth last appear in a Leinster Under-21 Football Final?
    a) 1992   b) 2002   c) 2012

Answers to Quiz 86: Longford

1. Damien Sheridan	11. Brian Kavanagh
2. Four	12. Kenagh
3. Pádraig Gearty	13. Mick Higgins
4. Glen Ryan	14. 2010
5. Dessie Barry	15. Fr. Manning Gaels
6. Martin Skelly	16. Brendan and Paul Barden
7. Liam Tierney	17. Dylan Quinn
8. Bobby Burns	18. Eamonn Coleman
9. Seán Murray	19. c) Abbeylara
10. Longford Slashers	20. b) 4

DIFFICULT

Quiz 88: Mayo

1. Can you name the Castlebar Mitchels player who received a black card in the opening minutes of the 2014 All-Ireland Club Championship Final?

2. Which Mayo club won a five-in-a-row of Mayo Senior Hurling Championships from 2008 to 2012?

3. How many Connacht Senior Football Championships did Mayo win during the 1970s?

4. Can you name the Mayo player who in 1948 became the first man to score a penalty in an All-Ireland Final?

5. Before 2009, when did Mayo last defeat Galway in Pearse Stadium in the Connacht Senior Championship?

6. Can you name the Mayo All-Ireland winner who was elected to the Dáil in the 1954 general election?

7. Who scored Mayo's only goal in the 2013 All-Ireland Senior Football Final?

8. Which county did Mayo beat in the 1936 All-Ireland Football Final?

9. Ray Prendergast Memorial Park is the home of which Mayo club?

10. How many All-Ireland Finals did John Maughan lose as Mayo manager?

11. Can you name the Mayo forward who scored two goals in the 2006 All-Ireland Final and who won an All-Star Award 13 years before?

12. Who are the only Mayo brothers to have won All-Star Awards?

13. In which year were Mayo substitutes Willie Casey, Paddy Jordan, and Mick Loftus awarded their 1951 All-Ireland medals?

14. Who was the Mayo goalkeeper in the 1989 All-Ireland Final?

Answers – page 183

15. Which journalist wrote the book *House of Pain, Through the Rooms of Mayo Football*?

16. Which county did Mayo beat in the 2013 All-Ireland Semi-Final?

17. Can you name the Mayo player who had his jaw broken in an off-the-ball incident during the 1985 All-Ireland Semi-Final against Dublin?

18. Can you name the Mayo club that won the All-Ireland Club Football Championship in 2005?

19. Before 2013, when did Mayo last win the All-Ireland Minor Football Championship?
    a) 1981
    b) 1983
    c) 1985

20. In which country was James Horan born?
    a) Argentina
    b) South Africa
    c) New Zealand

Answers to Quiz 87: Louth

1. Stefan White
2. Carlton
3. Eddie Boyle
4. JP Rooney
5. Westmeath
6. Four
7. 1910
8. Paddy Keenan
9. Clan na Gael
10. 1960
11. Séamus Flood
12. Benny Gaughran
13. Geraldines
14. Patsy Coleman
15. St. Joseph's
16. Seán Óg Flood
17. Mattock Rangers
18. Stephen White
19. b) Knockbridge
20. c) 2012

DIFFICULT

Quiz 89: Meath

1. Who succeeded Seán Boylan as Meath manager in 2005?

2. Which Meath player was sent off in the 1988 All-Ireland Final replay?

3. Who captained Meath in the 2001 All-Ireland Final?

4. In which year did St. Pat's win the Hogan Cup for the first time?

5. How many All-Star Awards did Martin O'Connell win during his career?

6. Which former Meath footballer was knicknamed 'The Boiler'?

7. Which club won the Meath Senior Football Championship for the first time in 2003?

8. In which county was Meath footballer Colm O'Rourke born?

9. How many times did Seán Boylan win the National Football League as a manager?

10. Can you name the former Meath player who acted as an adviser to the successful Down team of the early 1960s?

11. Can you name the Meath hurler who captained the Royals to Nicky Rackard Cup success in 2009?

12. All-Ireland Kick Fada champions Mary Sheridan, Gillian Bennett, and Gráinne Nulty play for which Meath club?

13. Which Meath official served as county board chairman for twenty years from 1949?

14. Which Meath club has won the Senior Hurling Championship the most times?

15. Can you name the Meath All-Ireland winner who played in the 1994 Connacht Championship for London?

Answers – page 185

16. Which Meath club hosts the Annual Road Hurling Championships?

17. Can you name the Meath father and son who won All-Ireland medals in the 1960s and the 1990s?

18. Can you name the only Meath player to be selected to the GAA Team of the Century in 1984?

19. Which Meath forward was selected as Texaco Footballer of the Year in 1987?
    a) Bernard Flynn
    b) Colm O'Rourke
    c) Brian Stafford

20. In which year did Meath win the All-Ireland Under-21 Football Championship?
    a) 1989   b) 1991   c) 1993

Answers to Quiz 88: Mayo

1. Richie Feeney
2. Ballyhaunis
3. None
4. Pádraig Carney
5. 1967
6. Henry Kenny
7. Andy Moran
8. Laois
9. Ballintubber
10. Three
11. Kevin O'Neill
12. Kenneth and Conor Mortimer
13. 2006
14. Gabriel Irwin
15. Keith Duggan
16. Tyrone
17. John Finn
18. Ballina Stephenites
19. c) 1985
20. c) New Zealand

DIFFICULT

183

Quiz 90: Monaghan

1. Who scored the equalizing free for Monaghan in the 1985 All-Ireland Semi-Final against Kerry?

2. Can you name the Monaghan ladies' footballer who has won seven All-Star Awards?

3. Which Monaghan club won the Ulster Senior Club Football Championship in 1986 and 1991?

4. In which year did Monaghan win the All-Ireland Junior Football Championship?

5. Who was the Meath player who deflected Paul Finlay's late free into his own net to give Monaghan victory in the 2005 Division 2 Final?

6. Monaghan greats John Rice and Hughie McKearney played with which club?

7. Can you name the Monaghan player who was the first Ulster goalkeeper to be awarded an All-Star Award?

8. Which Monaghan forward did Tyrone's Seán Cavanagh pull down during their 2013 All-Ireland Quarter-Final clash?

9. Who was the first Monaghan man to be elected President of the GAA?

10. Which county did Monaghan defeat in the 1985 National League Final?

11. Which Monaghan man captained UCD to Sigerson Cup success in 1974?

12. Who captained Monaghan to the Ulster title in 2013?

13. Brothers Pat and Séamus McEnaney played for which Monaghan club?

14. If you lived in Newbliss, which would be your local GAA club?

15. Can you name the Monaghan woman who served as president of the Camogie Association from 1985 to 1988?

16. Can you name the Monaghan player who scored a penalty against Kerry in the 2007 All-Ireland Quarter-Final?

17. Can you name the Monaghan man who won Junior, Intermediate, and Senior Championship medals with three different clubs?

18. In which position did Eugene 'Nudie' Hughes win his first All-Star Award in 1979?

19. In which year did Monaghan first appear in an All-Ireland Final?
    a) 1930   b) 1940   c) 1950

20. What did Kieran Finlay score for Monaghan in the 1979 Ulster Final?
    a) 2–5   b) 1–7   c) 1–9

Answers to Quiz 89: Meath

1.	Éamonn Barry	11.	Neil Hackett
2.	Gerry McEntee	12.	Seneschalstown
3.	Trevor Giles	13.	Fr. Patrick Tully
4.	2000	14.	Kilmessan
5.	Four	15.	Ollie Murphy
6.	Tommy McGuinness	16.	Boardsmill
7.	Blackhall Gaels	17.	Pat and Paddy Reynolds
8.	Leitrim	18.	Paddy O'Brien
9.	Three	19.	c) Brian Stafford
10.	Peter McDermott	20.	c) 1993

DIFFICULT

Quiz 91: Offaly

1. Can you name the Offaly man who refereed a total of five All-Ireland Finals, three in hurling and two in football?

2. Which of the Dooley brothers won the most All-Stars?

3. Can you name the Offaly man who captained UCG to Fitzgibbon Cup success in 1977?

4. Can you name the Offaly club that has produced two All-Ireland-winning football captains?

5. Up to 2014, how many All-Ireland Senior Club Hurling Championships has Birr won?

6. Can you name the two Offaly players who won an All-Ireland Minor Hurling Championship in 1989 and a Leinster Football Championship in 1997?

7. Who was the Offaly goalkeeper in the 1995 All-Ireland Hurling Final?

8. What is the name of the hurling club based around Ferbane?

9. Who resigned as Offaly Senior Football manager after only five weeks in the job during the 2000s?

10. Who wrote the book *Kings of September – The Day Offaly Denied Kerry Five in a Row*?

11. In which year did Offaly win the National Hurling League for the first time?

12. Which Offaly club won its first Senior Hurling Championship in 2012?

13. Who was known as 'The iron man from Rhode'?

14. Can you name the Offaly man who captained Leinster to Railway Cup success in 1962?

15. Who managed the Offaly camogie team to All-Ireland Junior success in 2009?

16. Can you name the Offaly player who scored two goals in the 1997 Leinster Football Final?

17. Can you name the player-manager who was central to Tullamore's 2009 Senior Hurling Championship success?

18. Can you name the Offaly dual player who was full-back on the 1998 National League winning team and later that year won an All-Ireland Hurling medal?

19. How many Leinster Senior Hurling Championships did Offaly win during the 1980s?
a) 5
b) 6
c) 7

20. Out of a total of 3–16 in the 1994 All-Ireland Hurling Final, how much did the Dooley brothers score between them?
a) 1–12
b) 2–8
c) 2–11

Answers to Quiz 90: Monaghan

1. Éamonn McEneaney
2. Jenny Greenan
3. Castleblayney Faughs
4. 1956
5. Mark Ward
6. Clontibret O'Neills
7. Paddy Linden
8. Conor McManus
9. Seán McCague
10. Armagh
11. Paddy Kerr
12. Owen Coyle
13. Corduff
14. Killeevan Shamrocks
15. Mary Lynch
16. Tomás Freeman
17. Tony Loughman
18. Corner-back
19. a) 1930
20. c) 1–9

DIFFICULT

Quiz 92: Roscommon

1. Can you name the Roscommon full-forward who was selected to the 1985 All-Star Team?

2. Can you name the Roscommon club that won the 1977 Connacht Hurling Club Championship?

3. Roscommon man Des Newton won a Provincial Championship with which county?

4. Which was the first Roscommon club to win the All-Ireland Club Football Championship?

5. In which year did Roscommon win the National Football League?

6. Which Roscommon club won the Senior Football Championship in 2008 and 2009?

7. The Connacht Under-21 Football Cup is named after which former Roscommon official?

8. Former Roscommon footballer Frankie Dolan won club championships with Roscommon and which other county?

9. Name the Roscommon player who lifted the Nestor Cup as Roscommon captain in 2010?

10. Starting in 1984, how many consecutive Connacht Senior Club Championships did Clann na nGael win?

11. Who scored Roscommon's late goal against Mayo in the 2001 Connacht Final?

12. In which year did Chris O'Dowd play for Roscommon in a Connacht Minor Football Final?

13. Which Roscommon club plays its home games at Orchard Park?

14. Can you name the Roscommon All-Ireland winner who was a TD from 1948 to 1965?

15. For which club does former Roscommon All-Star Francie Grehan play?

16. Can you name the Roscommon player who broke the crossbar during the 1962 Connacht Final?

17. Can you name the Roscommon man who won the 2009 All-Ireland Poc Fada Championship?

18. Who was the Roscommon goalkeeper in the 1980 All-Ireland Football Final?

19. How many Connacht Senior Football Championships did Tony McManus win with Roscommon?
    a) 4   b) 5   c) 6

20. In which year was Dr. Hyde Park officially opened?
    a) 1951   b) 1961   c) 1971

Answers to Quiz 91: Offaly

1. John Dowling
2. Johnny
3. Pat Fleury
4. Walsh Island
5. Four
6. Finbarr Cullen and Seán Grennan
7. David Hughes
8. Belmont
9. Richie Connor
10. Michael Foley
11. 1991
12. Kilcormac/Killoughey
13. Paddy McCormack
14. Greg Hughes
15. Joachim Kelly
16. Roy Malone
17. Kevin Martin
18. John Ryan
19. b) 6
20. c) 2–11

DIFFICULT

Quiz 93: Sligo

1. In which year did Institute of Technology, Sligo, win the Sigerson Cup for the first time?

2. Who was secretary of the Sligo County Board from 1970 to 2007?

3. Can you name the former Offaly footballer who was appointed manager of the Sligo Senior Football Team in 2013?

4. Which former All-Star was part of 1975 Sligo management team?

5. Can you name the former Mayo player who transferred to Sligo during the 2000s?

6. What colours does Castleconnor wear?

7. Who was the Enniscrone/Kilglass referee who refereed the 2009 All-Ireland Football Final?

8. In which year did Éamonn O'Hara make his senior debut for Sligo?

9. Can you name the Sligo player who won an All-Star Award in 2010?

10. With which club does Sligo footballer Adrian Marren play?

11. Up to 2013, which was the last Sligo club to win back-to-back Senior Football Championships?

12. The Connacht Minor Football Championship cup is named after which Sligo administrator?

13. Can you name the Sligo player who scored the equalizing point against Armagh in the drawn 2002 All-Ireland Quarter-Final?

14. Can you name the former Republic of Ireland soccer international who scored two goals for Sligo in a National League Quarter-Final against Kerry?

15. Which is the only Sligo club to win the Connacht Club Football Championship?

16. Sligo became the first men's intercounty team to have its kit made by which manufacturer in 2014?

17. Can you name the Sligo man who captained UCG to Sigerson Cup success in 1963?

18. Who was the sponsor of the Sligo team when they won the Connacht Championship in 2007?

19. How many points did Sligo score against Galway in the 2000 Connacht Senior Football Championship?
    a) 2   b) 3   c) 4

20. In which year during the 2000s did Sligo revert to wearing predominantly black jerseys?
    a) 2000   b) 2001   c) 2002

Answers to Quiz 92: Roscommon

1. Paul Earley
2. Tremane
3. Donegal
4. St. Brigid's
5. 1979
6. Castlerea St. Kevin's
7. JJ Fahy
8. Longford
9. Peter Domican
10. Six
11. Gerry Lohan
12. 1997
13. Elphin
14. Jack McQuillan
15. St. Aidan's
16. Aidan Brady
17. Gerry Fallon
18. Gay Sheerin
19. c) 6
20. c) 1971

DIFFICULT

Quiz 94: Tipperary

1. With which Tipperary club did Republic of Ireland soccer player Shane Long play?

2. By what nickname was former Tipperary hurler Mickey Byrne known?

3. In which year did Tipperary win the All-Ireland Camogie Championship for the first time?

4. Tipperary scored four goals in the 2010 All-Ireland Hurling Final. Lar Corbett scored three; who got the fourth?

5. Which Tipperary club plays its home games at Lacken Park?

6. Who scored Tipperary's late winning goal in the 2011 All-Ireland Minor Football Final?

7. In which year did Mick Murphy captain Tipperary to All-Ireland success?

8. Can you name the Tipperary goalkeeper who won five All-Ireland Camogie Championships?

9. Which Tipperary club won the All-Ireland Senior Club Hurling Championship in 1987?

10. Can you name the Tipperary man who contested four All-Ireland Minor Hurling Championship Finals?

11. Which Tipperary club was the first to win a Senior Football and Hurling Championship double in the same year?

12. Which Tipperary GAA Club represents the areas of Clougheen and Burncourt?

13. Can you name the Tipperary brothers who between them won four consecutive All-Star Awards from 1986 to 1989?

14. Who was the Tipperary hurling manager from 1994 to 1996?

15. Can you name the Tipperary substitute who scored two goals in the 1987 Munster Senior Hurling Final replay against Cork?

16. With which club did Tipperary hurler Pat Fox play?

17. With which Tipperary club did musician Christy Moore play football during the 1960s?

18. Can you name the Tipperary referee who took charge of the 1994 and 2000 All-Ireland Hurling Finals?

19. How many goals did Tipperary score in the 1951 All-Ireland Hurling Final?
a) Seven   b) Eight   c) Nine

20. How many Munster Senior Hurling Championships did Tipperary win during the 1990s?
a) Two   b) Three   c) Four

Answers to Quiz 93: Sligo

1. 2002
2. Tom Kilcoyne
3. Pat Flanagan
4. Brian McEniff
5. Alan Costello
6. Red and white
7. Marty Duffy
8. 1994
9. Charlie Harrison
10. Curry
11. St. Patrick's, Dromard
12. Tom Kilcoyne
13. Dara McGarty
14. Seán Fallon
15. St. Mary's
16. Kukri
17. Hugh McGonigle
18. Clifford Electrical
19. c) 4
20. b) 2001

DIFFICULT

Quiz 95: Tyrone

1. Who was Tyrone Senior Football Manager from 1996 to 1998?

2. With which club did Cormac McAnallen play his club football?

3. Can you name the Tyrone man who captained Queen's University to Sigerson Cup success in 1971?

4. Which Tyrone club won a three-in-a-row of Senior Hurling Championships from 2006 to 2008?

5. Who was the first Tyrone man to win an All-Star Award?

6. With which club did Plunkett Donaghy play?

7. Who scored Tyrone's only goal in the 2008 All-Ireland Football Final?

8. Which Tyrone club plays its home matches in Gardrum Park?

9. In which year did Tyrone win the Ulster Senior Football Championship for the first time?

10. Which county did Tyrone beat in the 1986 All-Ireland Senior Football Semi-Final?

11. Who captained Tyrone in the 1995 All-Ireland Senior Football Final?

12. How many All-Star Awards did Peter Canavan win during his career?

13. Who knocked Tyrone out of the 2002 All-Ireland Championship?

14. Can you name the Tyrone player who won an Ulster Minor, Under-21, and Senior Championship with Tyrone in 1973?

15. How many championship matches did Tyrone play during the 2005 season?

16. In which year did Tyrone reach the All-Ireland Ladies' Football Final for the first time?

17. After which former Tyrone footballer is the Man of the Match Award in the MacRory Cup Final named?

18. Up to 2013, how many Ulster Senior Football Championships has Mickey Harte won as manager of Tyrone?

19. Who was Tyrone's top scorer in the 2008 All-Ireland Final?
    a) Brian Dooher
    b) Seán Cavanagh
    c) Colm McCullagh

20. How many points did Tyrone concede against Kerry in the 2003 All-Ireland Semi-Final?
    a) 4   b) 6   c) 8

Answers to Quiz 94: Tipperary

1.	Gortnahoe-Glengoole	11.	Loughmore-Castleiney
2.	The Rattler	12.	Fr. Sheehys
3.	1999	13.	Bobby and Aidan Ryan
4.	Noel McGrath	14.	Fr. Tom Fogarty
5.	Newport	15.	Michael Doyle
6.	Colman Kennedy	16.	Éire Óg Annacarty
7.	1964	17.	Clonmel Commercials
8.	Jovita Delaney	18.	Willie Barrett
9.	Borris-Ileigh	19.	a) Seven
10.	Jimmy Doyle	20.	a) Two

DIFFICULT

Quiz 96: Waterford

1. Can you name the Waterford player who was sent off in the 1998 Munster Senior Hurling Final replay?

2. In which year did Waterford win the Munster Under-21 Football Championship for the first time?

3. Who managed Waterford to All-Ireland Minor Hurling success in 2013?

4. Which Waterford club won the Senior Hurling Championship for the first time in 2013?

5. Can you name the Waterford man who was President of the GAA from 1952 to 1955?

6. The under-age teams of which club are known as 'Sacred Heart'?

7. Name Waterford's all-time top scorer in championship hurling.

8. Can you name the former Waterford footballer who managed a county in a provincial final during the 2000s?

9. Who is the only Waterford native to have captained Waterford IT to Fitzgibbon Cup success?

10. Which Waterford club was the first to compete in an All-Ireland Senior Club Hurling Final?

11. Can you name the Waterford GAA administrator who served as President of the GAA from 1970 to 1973?

12. Which former Waterford football manager was better known as 'Jackson'?

13. Which county did Waterford defeat in the 1948 All-Ireland Hurling Final?

14. In which year did Dungarvan Colleges win the Dr. Croke Cup for the first time?

Answers – page 199

15. How many All-Star Awards did John Mullane win during his career?

16. Who managed the Waterford Ladies' Football Team to five All-Ireland Championships during the 1990s?

17. Which club won its first ever Waterford Senior Football Championship in 1998?

18. Can you name the player who scored three goals for Waterford in the 2007 Munster Senior Hurling Final?

19. In which year did Tony Browne make his Waterford senior debut?
    a) 1989   b) 1991   c) 1993

20. Who scored Waterford's only goal in the 2008 All-Ireland Senior Hurling Final?
    a) John Mullane   b) Eoin McGrath   c) Eoin Kelly

Answers to Quiz 95: Tyrone

1. Danny Ball
2. Eglish St. Patrick's
3. Patrick Park
4. Éire Óg Carrickmore
5. Kevin McCabe
6. Moy
7. Tommy McGuigan
8. Dromore St. Dympna's
9. 1956
10. Galway
11. Ciarán Corr
12. Six
13. Sligo
14. Frank McGuigan
15. Ten
16. 2010
17. Iggy Jones
18. Four
19. b) Seán Cavanagh
20. b) 6

DIFFICULT

Quiz 97: Westmeath

1. Which club was the first Westmeath winner of the Leinster Senior Football Club Championship?

2. Which former Westmeath hurler had the knickname 'Jobber'?

3. Can you name the Westmeath man who captained DCU to Sigerson Cup success in 2012?

4. With which club does former Westmeath goalkeeper Gary Connaughton play?

5. Which Westmeath school has won the Hogan Cup on three occasions?

6. Can you name the Westmeath GAA administrator who became President of the Ladies' Gaelic Football Association in 2003?

7. Who was manager of the Westmeath Minor Football Team that contested the 2013 Leinster Final?

8. Can you name the only two Westmeath players to start the 1995 All-Ireland Minor Final and the 1999 Under-21 Final?

9. Who is the only Westmeath man with two All-Star Awards?

10. Whom did Páidí Ó Sé succeed as Westmeath manager in 2003?

11. Can you name the Westmeath handballer who in 2014 became the first man to win a Senior All-Ireland in all four codes of handball: 60 x 30, 40 x 20, Hardball, and One-Wall?

12. Which Westmeath club was known as Mental Hospital GAA Club until the late 1950s?

13. Can you name the Westmeath man who was chosen as a dual replacement All-Star in 1982?

14. Can you name the Westmeath footballer who was cleared by a high-court ruling to play in the 2004 Leinster Final?

15. Can you name the Limerick All-Ireland winner who managed the Westmeath hurling team?

16. Collinstown, Fore, Glenidan, and Rickardstown hurling clubs amalgamated in 1969 to form which current Westmeath club?

17. In which year did Westmeath win the Christy Ring Cup for the first time?

18. What was the name of the fly-on-the-wall documentary that followed Westmeath manager Páidí Ó Sé during his first year in charge of the county?

19. In which year did Westmeath win the All-Ireland Under-21 Football Championship for the first time?
    a) 1987
    b) 1994
    c) 1999

20. Which club has won the Westmeath Senior Football Championship the most times?
    a) Garrycastle
    b) Athlone
    c) Mullingar Shamrocks

Answers to Quiz 96: Waterford

1. Michael White	11. Pat Fanning
2. 2003	12. John Kiely
3. Seán Power	13. Dublin
4. Passage	14. 2013
5. Vincent O'Donoghue	15. Five
6. Erin's Own	16. Michael Ryan
7. Paul Flynn	17. St. Saviour's
8. Jason Ryan	18. Dan Shanahan
9. Kevin Moran	19. b) 1991
10. Mount Sion	20. c) Eoin Kelly

DIFFICULT

Quiz 98: Wexford

1. Which former Wexford hurler wrote the book *No Hurling at the Dairy Door*?

2. Can you name the Kerry All-Ireland winner who managed the Wexford footballers during the 1990s?

3. With which club did Wexford dual player Redmond Barry play?

4. In which year did Oulart-the-Ballagh win the Wexford Senior Hurling Championship for the first time?

5. Which Wexford hurler won the Texaco Hurler of the Year Award in 1976?

6. Former Wexford manager Liam Griffin played Under-21 hurling with which county?

7. Former Wexford manager Pat Roe is a native of which county?

8. Which is the most northerly club in Wexford?

9. Can you name the Wexford club that has won All-Ireland Senior Hurling and Camogie Championships?

10. In which year did Wexford win the All-Ireland Senior Hurling Championship, the Leinster Senior Championship, and the National Hurling League?

11. Can you name the Wexford player who scored a goal against Kilkenny in both the 1996 and 1997 Leinster Senior Hurling Championship?

12. Can you name the Wexford brothers who started the 1996 All-Ireland Senior Hurling Final?

13. Can you name the London GAA Club with strong Wexford connections?

14. Can you name the Wexford man with the most All-Star Awards?

15. Which Wexford club plays its home matches at Tom Somers Park?

16. Can you name the Wexford hurler who is the all-time top goalscorer in championship hurling with 59 goals?

17. Can you name the Wexford footballer who played soccer in England with Preston North End during the 2000s?

18. Name the Wexford player who was sent off in the 1996 All-Ireland hurling final.

19. Who captained the Wexford Camogie team to All-Ireland success in 2007?
    a) Mary Leacy
    b) Una Leacy
    c) Ursula Jacob

20. By how many points did Wexford trail at half-time in its 2008 Leinster Championship match against Meath before winning by one point?
    a) 6   b) 8   c) 10

Answers to Quiz 97: Westmeath

1. Garrycastle
2. John McGrath
3. Kieran Gavin
4. Tubberclair
5. Carmelite College, Moate
6. Geraldine Giles
7. Tommy Carr
8. Fergal Murray and Shane Deering
9. John Keane
10. Luke Dempsey
11. Robbie McCarthy
12. St. Loman's
13. Willer Lowery
14. Rory O'Connell
15. Tom Ryan
16. Lough Lene Gaels
17. 2005
18. *Marooned*
19. c) 1999
20. b) Athlone

DIFFICULT

Quiz 99: Wicklow

1. Which future All-Ireland Senior Football winner won a Leinster Championship with the Wicklow Vocational Schools team during the 1980s?

2. Who succeeded Mick O'Dwyer as Wicklow manager in 2011?

3. Which Wicklow club won the 2011 Leinster Intermediate Club Football Championship?

4. Can you name the former Wicklow footballer who was a selector with the Ireland International Rules team in 2008?

5. Which Wicklow GAA club is known as the 'Billies'?

6. The winners of the Wicklow Senior Football Championship receive which cup?

7. Can you name the Wicklow man who won the 1997 and 2000 All-Ireland Poc Fada Championship?

8. Former GAA President Jack Boothman is a member of which Wicklow club?

9. In which year did Kevin O'Brien win his All-Star Award?

10. In which village is An Tóchar the local GAA club?

11. Who was the manager of the Wicklow Senior Hurling team that won the All-Ireland B Championship in 2003?

12. Up to the 1930s, what was the predominant colour of the Wicklow jerseys?

13. For which hurling club does Wicklow dual star Leighton Glynn play?

14. In which year did St. Mary's win the Wicklow Senior Football Championship for the first time?

15. Can you name the Wicklow native who won an All-Ireland medal with Dublin in 1963?

16. The O'Byrne Cup is named after Wicklow official Matt Byrne, who was involved with which club?

17. Which Wicklow club hosts the annual All-Ireland Kick Fada Championships in September?

18. Can you name the Wicklow referee who was famously bundled into the boot of a car after officiating an Under-21 Football match during the 1980s?

19. Which county did Wicklow defeat in the 2007 Final of the Tommy Murphy Cup?
    a) Louth
    b) Sligo
    c) Antrim

20. Which Wicklow club has won the Senior Hurling Championship on the most occasions?
    a) Glenealy
    b) Carnew Emmets
    c) Avondale

Answers to Quiz 98: Wexford

1. Billy Rackard
2. Jo Jo Barrett
3. St. Anne's
4. 1994
5. Tony Doran
6. Clare
7. Laois
8. Kilanerin-Ballyfad
9. Buffers Alley
10. 1956
11. Billy Byrne
12. John and George O'Connor
13. Fr. Murphy's
14. Martin Quigley
15. Gusserane
16. Nicky Rackard
17. Ciarán Lyng
18. Éamonn Scallan
19. a) Mary Leacy
20. c) 10

DIFFICULT

Quiz 100: Pot Luck

1. Can you name the Tipperary player who won an All-Ireland medal in the 1980s, 1990s, and 2000s?

2. Can you name the player with a provincial football medal and a European Under-18 Soccer Championship medal?

3. In which year was the qualifier system introduced in football?

4. The DVD *Total Faith* featured which county's journey to All-Ireland success?

5. Which club has provided more All-Ireland-winning hurling captains than any other?

6. Rory McIlroy's uncle Mickey McDonald played intercounty football with which county during the 1980s?

7. Séamus 'Cheddar' Plunkett is the current manager of which intercounty hurling team?

8. For which Westmeath club did singer Bressie play?

9. For which Dublin club did Ireland rugby international Luke Fitzgerald play?

10. Can you name the Galway man who won an All-Ireland medal with Down during the 1960s?

11. Which Meath player missed a penalty in both the 1999 and 2001 All-Ireland Finals?

12. Can you name the only player not from either Kerry or Dublin who has won four All-Ireland Football medals since 1950?

13. Can you name the last Munster club to win the All-Ireland Club Football Championship?

14. What is the name of the cup that the winners of the International Rules Series receive?

15. Which is the most northerly GAA club in Ireland?

16. Which player did Mícheál Ó Muircheartaigh describe as 'the man who drives a JCB on a Monday and turns into one on a Sunday'?

17. In which year did Offaly win the All-Ireland Senior Football Championship for the first time?

18. Can you name the Cork player who scored his side's only goal in the five All-Ireland Finals they played from 1987 to 1990?

19. What age was Waterford hurler Tony Browne when he retired from intercounty hurling in 2014?
    a) 39
    b) 40
    c) 41

20. Which county has won the All-Ireland Ladies' Football Championship on the most occasions?
    a) Cork
    b) Kerry
    c) Waterford

Answers to Quiz 99: Wicklow

1. Larry Tompkins
2. Harry Murphy
3. Éire Óg, Greystones
4. Hugh Kenny
5. Ballymanus
6. Miley Cup
7. Colin Byrne
8. Blessington
9. 1990
10. Enniskerry
11. Michael Neary
12. Green
13. Glenealy
14. 2011
15. John Timmons
16. Baltinglass
17. Bray Emmets
18. Johnny Price
19. c) Antrim
20. b) Carnew Emmets

DIFFICULT

Keeping Score

Keeping Score

Keeping Score

Keeping Score

Keeping Score

Keeping Score

Keeping Score

Get quizzical with the Collins quiz range

NEW

NEW

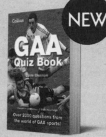

Available in paperback and ebook.

Available in paperback.

Available in paperback.

Available in paperback and ebook.

Available in paperback and ebook.

Available in paperback and ebook.

Available in paperback and ebook.

Available in paperback and ebook.

All **Collins** quiz range titles in paperback are RRP £6.99. Ebook prices may vary.

Available to buy from all good booksellers.

Follow us on Twitter 🐦 @collinsdict | Like us on Facebook 🅵 facebook.com/CollinsDictionary